THEOLOGY OF
HER BODY

Discovering the Beauty and Mystery of Femininity

JASON EVERT

ASCENSION
West Chester, Pennsylvania

Ascension
PO Box 1990
West Chester, PA 19380
1-800-376-0520
ascensionpress.com

Cover design: Devin Schadt

Printed in the United States of America
24 25 26 27 28 5 4 3 2 1

ISBN 978-1-954882-45-4 (paperback)
ISBN 978-1-954882-46-1 (e-book)

CONTENTS

FOREWORD

Perhaps you are wondering why a guy has written a book for women called *Theology of Her Body.* And here is another guy writing the foreword.

Obviously, Jason Evert and I can't speak about women with the authority that a woman can. But we do speak as men who have devoted our lives to understanding, upholding, and defending the dignity of women. This is the mission of every man, but men have tragically let you down—individually and collectively.

It seems to me that women often find it difficult to embrace the gift of their femininity because of wounds caused by men who have failed to honor them. A world that portrays women as objects for male pleasure is a world that puts women on the defensive.

Before I go any further, allow me, as a representative of the male side of the human race, to say how deeply sorry I am for the ways that my lusts and the lusts of other men have wounded you. Allow me to say how deeply sorry I am for the failures of men to love you, to honor you, and to uphold and defend your dignity as a woman. These wounds go very deep in a woman's heart. Please forgive us.

But what if both women and men could come to understand more fully the divine treasures revealed through the mystery of woman? *Theology of Her Body,* by Jason Evert, certainly provides an excellent place to start.

In a series of 129 talks, St. John Paul II set out to demonstrate the *beauty* of God's plan for sexual love and the joy of living it. He called this new vision of sex, love, and the human person the

Theology of the Body (TOB). To say "theology of the body" is simply another way of saying "made in the image of God." This means that our bodies are not only *biological;* they are also (and even more so) *theological.* Our bodies offer us, if we have eyes to see it, a profound "study of God." Just as a work of art points to the heart of the artist, so, too, does the human body point to the heart of the God who made us.

John Paul II's Theology of the Body talks themselves are scholarly. They need to be broken open if the average reader is to benefit from them. But beyond "translating" the TOB into a language average readers can understand, the various themes of John Paul II's talks must also be applied to real aspects of our lives.

This is what you're holding in your hands right now. In *Theology of Her Body* and (on the flip side) *Theology of His Body,* Jason Evert reflects with great wit and wisdom on certain aspects of John Paul II's TOB as they apply to the lives of young men and women. Through a creative application of some key principles found in John Paul II's Theology of the Body, Jason helps us to reclaim the true nature and dignity of femininity and, through that, the true nature and dignity of our humanity.

The world offers us a message about the meaning of femininity that is very different from the one you will find in this book. Listen to your heart, and ask yourself which message corresponds more to what you really yearn for. There are a lot of counterfeit "loves" on the market. You are worth the real deal. Don't settle for anything less.

–Christopher West
Theology of the Body Institute

INTRODUCTION

I was ready to send the manuscript of this book to the publisher when Ashley emailed me. She had just broken up with her boyfriend (the father of her four-year-old child) and was searching for hope. Memories of abuse, rape, and infidelity had marred her concept of relationships, but beneath the scars was a heart that still longed for authentic love. She decided to turn her life around, but wondered in her email, "Am I too far gone to be chaste and pure for my future spouse?" I offered her my encouragement and sent her the text you're now holding. She would be the first to read it. She soon emailed me, writing:

> It took me years of living in sin to destroy my life. It took five minutes to want it all back. I have never felt empowered as a woman until I read this. A woman's worth has never been so clear to me as it is now. I wanted to be better and live better, and you opened my eyes to what is really important and what God really wants for us. How could anyone not want what he has to give? If only more people knew. It is amazing what you can learn when you open your heart and your mind to something new.

Ashley was not raised in a religious home and only attended church periodically. She may have heard that she was made in the image and likeness of God. However, these words meant little to her. She understood that she had a soul, but she never considered the fact that God was also the architect of her body. For the first time, she began to see that God created the feminine form to reveal a woman's identity and her mission. Stamped into every woman's body is the sign that she is called to love and be loved.

But a woman's body isn't simply a revelation of femininity. Because women are made in the image and likeness of God, they also reveal something of heaven on earth. Thinking of a woman's body in this way may be new for you, and the frankness of what you're about to read may even shock you. But I hope that if you open your heart and mind like Ashley did, you will find as much consolation and encouragement as she did from reading these pages.

In the beginning …

We know from the book of Genesis that God created men and women "in his image and likeness." We know from the first letter of John that "God is love" (1 John 4:8). Therefore, men and women are made in the image and likeness of Love. This isn't hard to see. Look at the design of the male and female bodies. They are made for each other. In fact, neither one makes complete sense apart from the other. *The human body reveals our mission to love.*

However, our calling to love one another has often been warped by sin. Instead of giving, men often resort to taking. Instead of receiving the gift of life from a man, many women fear their own fertility. Others may not even believe they deserve to be loved. No one is free from the effects of sin, but God offers us all the hope of redemption. No matter how far we fall away from God's plan for our lives, we always bear in our own bodies a reminder of who we are called to become.

On the flip side of this book, *Theology of His Body,* I discuss how the man's body reveals his identity. His body reveals his strength and his call from God to initiate the gifts of love and life as a bridegroom and father. As a woman, your physical traits reflect different, feminine qualities. For example, you are made for relationships, you possess great beauty, and you have a deep element of mystery about you. All of this can be seen by looking at the way God created you. By studying the way God designed your body—and even your desires—you can learn who you are as a woman, how you should live, and who made you.

CHAPTER 1

A MYSTERY TO BE REVEALED

Have you ever asked someone a difficult question about religion, and because the person couldn't offer an adequate reply, he or she said, "I don't know. It's a mystery." You probably felt dissatisfied, as if the term "mystery" was supposed to explain everything that doesn't make sense. While it is true that the human mind cannot fully comprehend everything, this use of the word "mystery" gives the term a bad reputation. Saying something is a "mystery" does not imply that we cannot know *anything* about the matter, but rather that we cannot know *everything* about it.

A mystery could be defined as something partly hidden because of its great depth. Because of its greatness, it is not easily unveiled, but it still deserves to be pursued. This definition of a mystery can apply to God. He is veiled from our senses, but because of his greatness, he deserves to be pursued. This definition of mystery also applies to women.

By your very nature, you possess mystery. This quality of womanhood is revealed not only in a woman's personality but also in her body. Dr. Alice Von Hildebrand pointed out, "First of all, her intimate organs are hidden from sight: they are inside her body. What is hidden usually refers to something deep and mysterious: we hide secrets; we hide what is personal and intimate."[1]

By your very nature, you possess mystery.

A woman's body reveals profound truths about who she is as a person. Because she is made in the image and likeness of God, she reveals certain truths about God.

A Mystery Is Hidden and Set Apart

Even in the Bible—which is God's revelation of himself—the presence of the divine is often enshrouded in mystery.

An ideal example of this is the Holy of Holies in the Old Testament. This was the most sacred space for the Israelites. It was a section of their holy Temple that was hidden behind a veil to emphasize its sacredness, and only one sanctified priest could enter this sanctuary once a year. Within the Holy of Holies was the Ark of the Covenant, which contained the Ten Commandments, the staff of Aaron, and the manna from heaven. Because of its sacred contents and its association with the presence of God, the Ark was plated in and out with pure gold. Because of the tremendous religious value of the Holy of Holies and the Ark of the Covenant, they were set apart and hidden from all people except the high priest.

Although this may sound strange, God's purpose in veiling himself is not to hide from us but rather to reveal profound truths about himself. Similarly, when a woman veils her body with modest clothing, she is not hiding herself from men. On the contrary, she is revealing her dignity to them. In much the same way, when God veiled his glory from the Israelites, he taught us a profound truth about himself. He is holy. In fact, the term holy literally means "set apart."

Just as the presence of God in the Holy of Holies was hidden and set apart, the Bible speaks with the same awe about a woman's body. In the Bible's love story, the Song of Songs, the author refers to the woman's body as an enclosed garden:

You have ravished my heart, my sister, my bride; you have ravished my heart with one glance of your eyes, with one bead of your necklace. How beautiful is your love, my sister, my bride. How much better is your love than wine … [You are] a garden enclosed, my sister, my bride, a garden enclosed, a fountain sealed! (Song of Songs 4:9–10, 12, NAB).

The language used in this passage is rich in meaning. For example, the woman's body is called a garden enclosed. The purpose of it being shut is "to keep away those who do not have a right to be present."[2] As for the fountain being sealed, pure water was treasured among ancient civilizations, so wells were often sealed to prevent people from contaminating the water. One biblical commentator noted, "Springs of water were sometimes enclosed by a wall with a locked entrance in order to make them

inaccessible to intruders. The metaphor is obvious."[3] Like the Holy of Holies, the image of the locked garden and spring reveal that a woman's body is not unapproachable. Rather, she is available only to the one who is worthy.

Speaking of the wedding night, one wife said that a bride should be able to say to her husband:

Now that God has received our pledge to live our married life in his sight, I am granted the permission to give you the keys to this garden, and I trust that you will approach it with "fear and trembling" ... The bridegroom should be reminded that God's permission is required in order for him to penetrate into this sacred enclosure, and that he should do so with both reverence and gratitude.[4]

Such sexual imagery may strike certain people as inappropriate, immodest, and even scandalous. But we must recall that God is the Author of Sacred Scripture—and the Architect of our anatomy. He is the one who inspired erotic love poetry in the heart of the Bible (Song of Songs). He did this because he knows that our sexuality is not a dirty, unmentionable thing. Rather, it is meant to be a reflection of God's own plan for mankind—to be eternally united with him in love.

> Although our culture drives a wedge between what is sexual and what is sacred, God sees things differently.

Pope Benedict XVI wrote in his first letter as pope that the Song of Songs is "an expression of the essence of biblical faith: that man can indeed enter into union with God ... But this union is no mere fusion, a sinking in the nameless ocean of the Divine; it is a unity which creates love, a unity in which both God and man remain themselves and yet become fully one."[5] The sexual metaphor is unmistakable. When a husband and wife express the union that creates love, they remain fully themselves and yet become fully one. Although our culture drives a wedge between what is sexual and what is sacred, God sees things differently.

Some may struggle with this "spousal analogy" that compares the love of a man and woman with the love of God for us. Some may argue that such bold and even erotic language goes too far. The opposite, in fact, is true. Although all human analogies to describe the love between God and man are inadequate, St. John Paul II contended that the spousal analogy is the least inadequate. In other words, it is the best analogy we humans have to describe the bliss of eternal union with God.

A Mystery Is Worth Pursuing

A friend once told me the story of a hermit who lived atop a mountain in the wilderness. Rumors spread among the people who lived in the villages below that this man had the ability to reveal God to whomever he wished. Upon hearing this, one villager decided to test the legend for himself, and he made the trek to the peak. Upon meeting the hermit, he asked to see the face of God. The wise monk motioned to the young man to follow him. Together, they walked in silence through the woods. As the anticipation mounted, the two came upon a stream, and the hermit pointed into the water. The lad came close and peered down. Not seeing anything, he gave the hermit a puzzled look. The hermit urged him to look closer. When the young man drew near to the brook, the hermit grasped him by the back of the neck and thrust his head underwater. The man flailed his arms and attempted in vain to rise. The hermit's unexpected strength kept the man's face submerged until he began to panic for his life. At last, the hermit released his grip and pulled the man back to regain his breath. Gasping for air and unable to speak, the man looked with bewilderment at the hermit. Calmly, the elderly man said, "When you desire to know God with as much fervor as you desired that breath of air, you will find him."

Some may read this and think, "It sounds like God doesn't *want* us to find him. Why does he make it so difficult, anyway?" God is not complicated, and he is not hiding from us. On the contrary, he is simple and wants us to seek him with sincerity. When we do this, we will discover that he is the one who is pursuing us.

For example, in the book of the prophet Jeremiah, God invites us, "You will seek me and find me; when you seek me with all your heart, I will be found by you" (Jeremiah 29:13-14). He does not throw himself at us but will reveal himself to the one who pursues him with a sincere heart.

It is not much different in the case of a healthy male-female relationship. A man should pursue a woman with his whole heart and dedicate his entire life to her if he hopes that she will give herself to him. You may have noticed that every modern love story portrays the man as willing to make any sacrifice to win over the woman. But this is apparent not just in the romantic movies often loved by girls. Even testosterone-guy movies depict the same thing. Some may argue that those who write such storylines are guilty of promoting outdated gender stereotypes. But how romantic would a movie be if the man were indecisive, passive, wimpy, and indifferent when it came to pursuing his beloved? Something in our hearts finds that detestable.

There is a reason why women long for the thrill of being wanted, pursued, and cherished. There is a reason why a man longs to win the heart of a woman. A prime example of this can be found in the Old Testament, where we read how Jacob fell in love with Rachel. He longed for her with such determination that he gladly served her father for seven years in exchange for her hand in marriage. The Scriptures tell us that the years "seemed to him but a few days because of the love he had for her" (Genesis 29:20). After seven years, the father did not give her to Jacob, so he willingly waited seven more years.

While many women will appreciate the romantic notion of such love, they are often disappointed with the quality of modern guys. "Where are these knights in shining armor? The guys at my school harass every girl that walks by in the hallway and play video games when they're not busy telling degrading jokes. And the few guys who are decent don't have the guts to ask anyone out!"

What's a girl to do?

Instead of looking for the ideal man, become the ideal woman and let him look for you. Take your focus off the dating scene for a time, and pursue God with as much sincerity as you wish a guy would pursue you. As one high school girl said to me, "A woman should hide her heart in God, and a man must go there to find it." Another girl wrote, "A woman should be so hidden in Christ that a man has to see Christ just to see her."

When you do this, you will come to see that you are loved and desired by Love himself. You will see that Christianity is not a list of rules, but rather an encounter with a person who knows and loves you perfectly. As you allow his love to transform you, you will realize your tremendous worth, and you will become a persuasive force in teaching boys how to become the kind of men women truly deserve.

Mysteries Are to Be Revealed, Not Exposed

Have you ever heard someone say, "If God wants us to believe in him, why doesn't he just reveal himself?" It seems like a reasonable request, but it overlooks the fact that he did reveal himself, and we crucified him. What else does he need to do? Write a book about himself? He did that. Or maybe establish a visible institution to pass down his teachings with his own authority? He did that as well, through the Church. Despite these efforts on his part, some people argue that he has not done enough. More often than not, these are the same people who won't go to the trouble of going online to find the nearest church.

But is there merit in their argument?

God cannot be reduced to a philosophical argument or a scientific proof. He is a person and a Bridegroom. One woman noted:

Imagine a young suitor who arrives seeking the hand of a princess. After a period of exchanged glances and slain dragons, she invites him to visit. And so he does—bearing a three-volume tome detailing the reasons why she is compelled, by reason and by the threat of eternal unhappiness, to love him. Our initial reaction to this man would be laughter, but if, for some reason, we were forced to take him seriously, we would consider him a presumptuous, unromantic jerk.[6]

This is not God's way of dealing with us. In fact, he sometimes appears to be hiding, like the lover in the Song of Songs, peering through the lattices at his beloved (see Song of Songs 2:9). In this stanza of the great love poem, the lover watches his beloved, although she cannot fully see him. He calls to her, "Arise, my love, my dove, my fair one, and come away; for behold, the winter is past, the rain is over and gone. … Arise, my love, my fair one, and come away. O my dove, in the clefts of the rock, in the covert of the cliff, let me see your face, let me hear your voice, for your voice is sweet, and your face is comely" (Song of Songs 2:10-14). He is hiding and bidding her to come.

God is a lover, and lovers make proposals. Certainly, God could reveal his glory to us if he wished. So what is he waiting for? In his book *Heaven's Song,* Christopher West recounts a conversation St. Francis of Assisi had with God:

It is reported that St. Francis of Assisi once asked God to allow him to hear the music of heaven. The Lord told Francis he knew not what he asked, for the sheer glory of heaven's song would spell certain death. The persistent saint pleaded eagerly, "Can't I hear just one note?" God conceded. As the story goes, Francis awoke from his coma a few days later.[7]

The human heart—even a saintly one—is not yet ready to take in the majesty of heaven. It would be like trying to fit the entire ocean into a glass of water. As Pope Benedict XVI writes,

> Man was created for greatness—for God himself; he was created to be filled by God. But his heart is too small for the greatness to which it is destined. It must be stretched. [Augustine] uses a very beautiful image to describe this process of enlargement and preparation of the human heart. "Suppose that God wishes to fill you with honey [a symbol of God's tenderness and goodness]; but if you are full of vinegar, where will you put the honey?" The vessel, that is your heart, must first be enlarged and then cleansed, freed from the vinegar and its taste. This requires hard work and is painful, but in this way alone do we become suited to that for which we are destined.[8]

In order to be filled by God, we must first empty ourselves. We must do our part and allow God to do his. He has not failed to make himself available to us. If anything, we are the ones that rarely make ourselves available to him. He has given us a proposal, and we are free to accept or reject it. If we truly wish to see his glory revealed, we first need to accept his proposal.

Just as skeptics demand that God reveal his glory to prove himself, the modern culture tells women, "If your body is so great, show yourself!" The woman who understands her worth would resist such an invitation and reply, "Because of my value, I veil myself. My body was not given to me for the sake of exposing it to you. If I show too much, I wouldn't be revealing my true worth to you. I would be distracting you from what matters most."

Perhaps these sentiments were best expressed by a teenage girl who approached me after I spoke in Los Angeles. She said, "I don't mean to sound cocky, but I don't want to marry a guy unless he is worthy of my body." By this, she did not mean that she thought her figure was perfect. She meant that she

You choose how and to whom you will reveal yourself.

understood the value of being made in the image and likeness of God. She had no problem with the idea of revealing herself to a worthy spouse. But she saw no point in exposing herself to win the attention of boys or merely for the sake of feeling good about herself. She knew that modesty is the proper attitude of a woman who knows the value of her mystery. It is fitting, then, that St. John Paul II calls women "the master of your own mystery."[9] You choose how and to whom you will reveal yourself. Never forget: The Bible says that God has glory in what he conceals. So do you.

When a woman observes how God chooses to reveal himself, she learns the truth about herself: *Only a worthy spouse deserves to experience the glory of her unveiled mystery.*

The Fall of Mystery

Because of the effects of original sin, a woman may cast aside her mysterious nature and elect to receive passing satisfactions from those who also lack patience. Because she does not believe that she deserves to be pursued, she begins to pursue. Instead of waiting to reveal herself to the one who is worthy, she exposes herself to those who have no right to see her. This process may begin with immodesty in speech and dress, but it often progresses to sensual flirting and outright sexual aggressiveness. While such a woman may believe she is being confident and assertive, the only thing she is revealing is her insecurity. Because she does not realize her own great worth, she accepts being treated without reverence. Perhaps without realizing it, she becomes, in the words of one blunt woman, "walking entertainment for men."[10]

Sadly, the modern media saturates young women with the message that a girl's value is determined by a boy's reaction to her. Taking this message to heart, girls often use their bodies as a means to receive affirmation. Especially when a girl does not receive a sense of her worth from her family, she will seek it elsewhere. Such a young woman may even come to the point of hating her own body while using it to find love. In the words of Pope Benedict XVI, "This is hardly man's great 'yes' to the body. On the contrary, he now considers his body and his sexuality as the purely material part of himself, to be used and exploited at will ... The apparent exaltation of the body can quickly turn into a hatred of bodiliness."[11]

Such a fall does not happen in an instant. Girls today are raised in a pornographic culture where toy dolls and grade-schoolers' clothing train them to view their bodies as objects. When a girl turns on the television, every advertisement from french fries to deodorant is sexualized. Meanwhile, an endless stream of filtered and flawless female bodies awaits them whenever they scroll through social media.

Wendy Shalit comments on the effects of this phenomenon: "There is no longer any mystery or power to sex—it is just expected that everything will be sexual, and so nothing is. There is nothing to wait for, or to look forward to." She continues, "Someone who is almost naked in front of strangers ... has little left to reveal to her lover."[12]

While many women give in to sin by choosing to expose too much of what should be kept secret, others feel exposed against their own will. Through harassment and sexual abuse, a woman may come to feel as if the mystery she possesses has been trampled upon. Perhaps no better word describes what she feels than "violation." The image comes to mind of an obnoxious drunkard stumbling into the Holy of Holies. He does not deserve to be in the presence of the sacred. He has no right. Despite the sacrilege of what he has done, the holiest of sanctuaries would not have lost any of its dignity. Its value remains.

When the secret of a woman's deepest intimacies has been taken by force or seduction, she may assume that she has nothing left to offer, and she may begin acting accordingly. What she may not realize is that she has not revealed herself to anyone. The gift has not been given, because this would require her full consent. She still has herself to give. However, for her to give and receive love, she must realize that she has lost nothing of her dignity as a woman. Instead, the one who violated her has renounced his dignity as a man. After all, a woman's value does not come from her virginity. Rather, her sexuality has value because of her! No matter what has happened in the past, a woman still has herself to give.

The Redemption of Mystery

No matter how great they may seem, the wounds of sin and the confusion caused by it are not meant to defeat you. The wounds can be healed, and your desires can be redeemed. What was once a twisted form of seeking out love through immodesty can become, through modesty, a radiant invitation for authentic love. Despair can be transformed into hope when a woman discovers she has immeasurable value, regardless of her past.

> Despair can be transformed into hope when a woman discovers her immeasurable value, regardless of her past.

So much depends on whether or not you see the truth of who you are in the eyes of God. In the words of Dr. Alice Von Hildebrand, "If little girls were made aware of the great mystery confided to them, their purity would be guaranteed. The very reverence which they would have toward their own bodies would inevitably be perceived by the other sex. Men are talented at reading women's body language, and they are not likely to risk being humiliated when a refusal is certain. Perceiving women's modesty, they would take their cue and, in return, approach the female sex with reverence."[13]

God has entrusted you with the mission of being the master of your own mystery. The young men who frustrate you with their whistling and crude remarks need you to realize your dignity. But how can they appreciate your worth if you do not appreciate yourself? You deserve to be loved. Because of your tremendous worth, you should only reveal yourself to the man who is worthy to be your husband. Imagine how the world would be transformed if women embraced such a calling from God. The mystery of his intimate love would shine through his daughters.

CHAPTER 2

A RELATIONSHIP TO BE PURSUED

In the beginning, God said, "Let us make man in our image, after our likeness" (Genesis 1:26). Because the Trinity exists as a relationship of Persons—Father, Son, and Holy Spirit—and we are made in the image and likeness of God, this means that we are made to live in interpersonal relationships. St. John Paul II teaches that God is a "communion of persons" whose love generates life. The same can be said of man and woman. Their love creates life.

Our capacity to reveal the relational nature of God is especially apparent in women. If there has ever been a creature made for relationships, it is woman. Her capacity for being connected to others is unparalleled. From a guy's perspective, this is nowhere more obvious than in the fact that women do not even venture into a restroom without bringing company.

While men often determine the quality of their lives by their accomplishments, women more often define the quality of their lives by their relationships. A man feels a deep sense of defeat when he fails to achieve, and a woman feels a deep sense of angst and anxiety when her relationships are troubled. This generalization, like all generalizations, is imperfect. Men, too, desire quality relationships, and women also value personal achievement. However, it cannot be denied that women are endowed with a unique capacity to relate to others.

Nature vs. Nurture?

Some claim that such differences are not natural and are caused by cultural norms being imposed upon the sexes. One author of a women's studies textbook argues that the very concept of femininity is "patriarchal mind control."[14] Not long ago, I read of a mother who seemed to believe that males and females are fundamentally the same and that girls act differently only because they are raised differently. To apply her theory, she avoided imposing gender stereotypes on her young daughter. The mom was a bit surprised, after having bought the little girl several toy trucks, to find her tucking each of them into bed.[15] Yet another mother who gave her daughter unisex toys was surprised to see her daughter cuddling a fire truck in a baby blanket, saying, "Don't worry little truckie, everything will be all right."[16]

While feminism has rightly objected to unfair discrimination against women, some feminists go too far in their efforts to equate the sexes. Men and women are different, and modern brain research has confirmed this. In her book *The Female Brain*, Louann Brazening, MD, points out that when a boy is only eight weeks old in his mother's womb, a surge of testosterone kills off cells in the communication center of his brain, while growing more cells in the area of the brain dedicated to sex and aggressiveness.[17] In adolescence, the female brain will mature two to three years earlier than the male brain.[18] At this point, you are either thinking, *Well, that explains a lot!* or *Do we really need neuroscience to confirm this?*

Indeed, men have more than twice as much brain space devoted to the sexual drive. Meanwhile, the woman's brain has eleven percent more neurons in the language and hearing centers and is physically larger in the area that forms emotions and memories.[19] Even from the time she is in her mother's womb, the two hemispheres of a woman's brain are neurologically more connected than those of men. This gives the woman a superior ability to express her speech, thought, and emotions. A woman will speak almost three times as many words as a man per day (20,000 vs. 7,000) and has a greater capacity for reading emotions and expressing empathy.

Some of these characteristics appear as soon as a girl is born. Newborn females respond more to the human face and to the cries of another baby.[20] Female babies prefer babbling at people, while baby boys are perfectly content babbling at toys. Even at the age of one, a girl is better able than a boy to respond to those who appear sad or hurt.[21]

As a woman grows, her brain becomes more and more skilled at intuition, reading faces, and sensing the nuances and inflections in a person's voice. One brain researcher called the female brain an "emotion detector." She added, "Like an F-16 [the] female brain is a high-performance emotion machine—geared to tracking, moment by moment, the non-verbal signals of the innermost feelings of others. By contrast ... it's only when men actually see tears that they realize, viscerally, that something is wrong ... The typical male brain reaction to an emotion is to avoid it at all costs."[22]

As a male, I can confirm this. Earlier this week, I sat down on the couch with my wife to watch a home makeover show that she seemed to enjoy. Within the first six minutes of the show, two people had cried three separate times. My wife was engrossed in the plot, but it was altogether too much for me to process. My brain hurt, so I did what any empathetic man would do. I left the room to play with our dog. As a man, I have neither the capacity nor the desire to enter into the emotional anguish of someone who needs an interior decorator. However, women are equipped with the capacity to literally feel what another is feeling. They are able to enter into the emotions of another with much greater ease than men. Some scientists call this ability "mirroring."

God has endowed women with these gifts, which allow them to accept others in love. These gifts equip women to excel at many tasks—especially motherhood. However, this openness to receive another is not only revealed on a microscopic level or in her emotions. It is also plainly revealed in her body.

Openness

From the dawn of creation, the openness of women to others has been recognized as an essential element—and gift—of her nature. In the context of her sexuality, it is the openness of the woman to a man that allows her to bear life.

The same can be said of the spiritual life. God is the one who initiates the gift of supernatural life, and we must be open to receiving it. This is why the Church is called the bride of Christ. In his letter to the Ephesians, St. Paul writes: "'For this reason a man shall leave his father and mother and be joined to his wife, and the two shall become one flesh.' This is a great mystery, and I mean in reference to Christ and the Church" (Ephesians 5:31-32). Down through the ages, theologians have recognized that women are an "archetype," or model, of humanity in its relationship to God. In other words, the woman's body is an image of the soul's receptivity to God's love. Perhaps this explains why it seems there are always more women at church than men. Receiving comes more naturally to them.

Because the soul receives supernatural life from God, the model for all Christians is the Blessed Virgin Mary. As a result of her "yes," she literally bore Jesus' life within her. However, her role was not a merely passive one. She actively received. In the original Greek, her response to Gabriel, "Be it done unto me," is in the optative mood of the verb. This indicates that Mary joyfully embraced the will of God and his plan of salvation. For this reason, Mary is our model of openness and receptivity to God's will.

What the Song of Songs is to the Old Testament, Mary's annunciation is to the New Testament. Consider the following parallels:

- In the love poetry of the Song of Songs, the bridegroom courts his bride by saying, "Behold, you are beautiful, my love, behold, you are beautiful! Your eyes are doves behind your veil" (Song of Songs 4:1). How easily one could imagine God proclaiming the beauty of Mary with these same words!

- In the Song of Songs, the beloved one is a "queenly maiden" who is the "fairest among women" (see Song of Songs 7:1, 5:9) and in the Gospel of Luke, Our Lady is called the "handmaid of the Lord" who is "blessed … among women" (Luke 1:38, 42).

- The lover says to his beloved, "You are all fair, my love; there is no flaw in you … My dove, my perfect one, is only one … flawless to her that bore her" (Song of Songs 4:7, 6:9). So, too, is the Blessed Virgin Mary without flaw because she is sinless.

- The bridegroom beckons his bride, "'Open to me, my sister, my love, my dove, my perfect one'" (Song of Songs 5:2). In the New Testament, Mary is the perfect one who is invited to receive the life of God within her.

- In the Old Testament, the bride is a "rose," and she proclaims, "As a lily among brambles, so is my love among maidens" (Song of Songs 2:2). So, too, does Mary's love for God surpass the love of all other creatures—angelic and human.

Because of her openness to the will of God, Mary brought God to the world. This is the vocation of all women, and therefore every woman should look to Our Lady to fulfill her vocation to deliver God to the world. As St. Teresa Benedicta of the Cross (Edith Stein) writes, "Every woman who wants to fulfill her destiny must look to Mary as the ideal."[23] Like the beloved of the Old Testament Song of Songs and Mary in the New Testament, you are chosen, desired, and beautiful in the eyes of God.

Although you may feel ignored, undesirable, and flawed, this is not your identity. Open yourself to the unconditional love of God, and you will have his life within you. Resist the temptation to define yourself simply by the current status of your human relationships. In her book *The Thrill of the Chaste*, Dawn Eden writes, "A woman with the courage to step out into the unknown, risking temporary loneliness for a shot at lasting joy, is more than a 'single.' She's *singular*. Instead of defining herself by what she lacks—a relationship with a man—she defines herself by what she has: a relationship with God."[24]

The Fall of Relationships

As a result of the effects of sin or abuse, a woman's receptivity can be wounded, or she may reject it. Our culture provides all too many examples of wounded receptivity:

- Some women do not believe they are worthy to receive love because of their own personal sins. A friend once informed me that the girl he fell in love with broke up with him saying, "You're such a nice guy, but I don't deserve that. I only date jerks." He would have been faithful to her and treated her well, but she felt that such a guy deserved a girl with a better past. Sadly, she didn't hope for a better future.

> Every woman who wants to fulfill her destiny must look to Mary as the ideal.

- Many women who have suffered through sexual abuse no longer feel open toward men. Instead, they may shut men out of their lives. Considering what such women have experienced, no one can blame them for feeling the need to do this. It is a way to protect their hearts from further pain. Unfortunately, such women may come to despise vulnerability, seeing it not only as a threat but also as a weakness. When a woman reaches this point, she may distrust not only men but even God himself.

- Other women reject their gift of receptivity through the use of contraception. This is not simply a rejection of pregnancy, but a rejection of the way the woman is created. Taking drugs to prevent life implies that there is something problematic in the woman's body that must be fixed with chemicals. In God's eyes, the woman's body is perfectly made. If she becomes pregnant from having sex, this does not mean something went wrong physically. It means something went right.

- Should a woman become pregnant and turn to abortion as a solution, she displays the deepest rejection of receptivity. She rejects the gift of life after receiving it within her. Through pregnancy, a woman's body becomes a tabernacle of life. In the words of Dr. Alice Von Hildebrand, "God therefore 'touches' the female body in placing this new soul into the temple of her womb."[25] When the woman chooses to abort this life, she contradicts her deepest desires and even her identity. St. Theresa Benedicta of the Cross observes, "To cherish, guard, protect, nourish, and advance growth is her natural, maternal yearning."[26] This is not who a woman *should* be; it's who she *is*. A woman, by her very nature, is tender and loving. Therefore, abortion contradicts the very nature of womanhood. The pressures and fears that shape her decision to end her pregnancy are often unimaginable, and those who have chosen abortion deserve compassion and love instead of judgment and wrath. But part of loving these women is helping them to recognize the depth of the wound, so that it may be fully healed.

- Although it is not a sin to experience same-sex attractions, women who experience such desires are often encouraged by the world to identify themselves by such attractions. While the word "lesbian" describes the feelings she experiences, such labels fall woefully short of defining her as a person. Every woman who experiences such attractions is first and foremost a beloved daughter of God, and this is the deepest truth of her identity. Because one's actions flow from one's identity, it is crucial that every person find their sense of self in God rather than in their sexual urges. Modern minds have a difficult time understanding this because the media encourages sexual "experimentation," sexualizes all attractions (and even friendships), and assures young women that such behavior is harmless, healthy, and natural. On the contrary, St. John Paul II explains that "chastity is the sure way to happiness."

- Some women have great difficulty receiving the gift of their own womanhood from God. Those who experience gender dysphoria or who self-identify as "trans" often feel a discord between their bodies and their sense of self. As Abigail Shrier explains, "They sense a dangerous chasm lies between the unsteady girls they are and the glamorous women social media tells them they should be. Bridging that gap feels hopeless." Such individuals deserve compassion and love, but they also deserve to know that they were not born into the wrong body. They were born into the wrong culture, one that tells them they might need to hurt their body in order to be their authentic self.

If the life-giving love between a man and a woman is an icon, or "sign," of the love God has for us, you can be certain that the devil will do everything in his power to destroy that icon. Furthermore, we can be certain that if God said that it is not good for man to be alone, the devil will entice the woman to reject man. By removing the male–female relationship ordered according to God's plan, the devil wipes out the most fundamental icon of God's love on earth.

If the devil is not successful in getting a woman to reject receptivity and relationships, his only option is to entice her to make an idol out of the icon. He urges the woman to make relationships with men the essence of her life. Relationships cease to be a reflection of God's love; they become a substitute for it. The guy replaces God.

When these relationships become sexual before marriage, the woman is often broken from disappointment. Her body has made a promise that does not exist in reality. In the words of one young man, "Physically, it felt good, but emotionally it felt really awkward. I was worried that our relationship was now going to be a lot more serious than it was before. It was like, 'Now what is she going to expect from me?'"[27] Such confusion and hurt may cause a young woman to despair, thinking that she is unloved.

> There is no wound that cannot be healed.

Thankfully, Christ did not come to condemn but to save. He came to redeem not only our souls but even our deepest desires. There is no wound that cannot be healed, and there is no human longing that is not fulfilled in him.

The Redemption of Relationships

When a woman opens herself to love and is then wounded in her vulnerability, she may come to doubt that healing is possible. How is a woman, after having been hurt so deeply, able to open herself again to the prospect of love?

Her first step needs to be to trust God. Because he is always true and faithful, she has nothing to fear in giving her heart to him. As the Bible says, "Hope for good things, for everlasting joy and mercy. You who fear the Lord, love him, and your hearts will be made radiant. Consider the ancient generations and see: who ever trusted in the Lord and was put to shame? ... For as his majesty is, so also is his mercy" (Sirach 2:9–10, 18). Even if we turn away from him, he is still true to his promise. As St. Paul wrote, "If we are faithless, he remains faithful—for he cannot deny himself" (2 Timothy 2:13).

> You are loved not because of what you do, but because of who you are: his daughter.

Many people do not open themselves fully to God because they do not believe he will love them if they are not saints. These are often people who grew up in families where they had to win the approval of their parents in order to be loved. They learned that the only way to earn their parents' approval was to get straight A's, make the team, and behave like an angel. To these people, love seems conditional, based upon one's performance.

Thankfully, God does not operate on this system. You are loved not because of what you do, but because of who you are: his daughter. Therefore, Christianity is not primarily about making yourself perfect for God. If anything, it is allowing him to love you when you are most imperfect. Holiness is ultimately his gift to you, not your attempt to reach him. This thought should give you the confidence to follow the invitation of St. Francis, who said, "Hold back nothing of yourself for yourself so that he who gives himself totally to you may receive you totally."

As a woman opens herself to receiving the love of God, she will be more able to receive the love she deserves. Without a foundation of God's love, a woman is far more likely to fall for men who are unable to love her as God does. In other words, they "love" her for what she *does*, not for who she *is.*

Once a woman learns to trust in God and receive his love, she will also be better able to love others. Through opening herself to others in compassion, empathy, and tenderness, she will reflect God's love on earth.

CHAPTER 3

A BEAUTY TO BE UNVEILED

Nothing on earth compares to the beauty of women. Such a statement may seem an exaggeration to some, but it is easy enough to prove. When was the last time you heard of someone who was addicted to looking at online pictures of sunsets? Could you imagine if guys in your school chuckled in glee as they sent pictures of waterfalls and flamingos to each other's cell phones? Despite how beautiful these other created things may be, just the thought of comparing them to the allure of a woman is absurd.

Nothing on earth compares to the beauty of women.

In the creation story of Genesis 2, the woman is the final work of God. She is the crescendo of creation. In the words of one perceptive woman:

> God gave Eve a beautiful form and a beautiful spirit. She expresses beauty in both. Better, she expresses beauty simply in who she is. Like God, it is her essence ... Eve just doesn't look right in a scene of brutal combat, or chopping a tree down. From time immemorial, when artists have tried to capture the essence of Eve, they have painted her at rest. There is no agenda here, no social stigmatizing or cultural pressure. This is true across all cultures and down through time. What have the artists seen that we have not? Eve speaks something different to the world than Adam does. Through her beauty. Beauty is powerful. It may be the most powerful thing on earth. It is dangerous. Because it matters.[28]

Advertisers are well aware of these facts. Researchers say that when a woman is pictured in an advertisement, both male and female viewers will look at the ad for fourteen to thirty percent longer.[29] She is captivating. Men simply don't have the same appeal. If advertisers want you to be allured by a product, why not place it in the hands of the most alluring creature on earth?

Unfortunately, because culture idolizes only sexualized beauty, many women don't realize that the beauty of a woman's body is not the only reason she is beautiful. Rather, her body is a revelation of her as a person. By looking at the woman, we can see who God has made her in every aspect of who she is. Her personality has beauty in the way she expresses compassion to others. Her voice is beautiful, especially when lifted to God in song. As a man, I can testify that even the smell of women is beautiful. If you doubt this, visit a college dormitory of women, and then visit an all-male dorm. The girl's dorm has the aroma of shopping mall soap and shampoo stores, while the guy's dorm smells like dirty laundry from a high school locker room.

The litany of beautiful qualities that women possess has been chronicled by poets and songwriters throughout history and will continue as long as women exist.

The Power of Beauty

When I went to college in Austria for a semester, I had the opportunity to visit some of the most breathtaking churches on earth. The memories of some of the cathedrals are indelibly imprinted upon my mind. I vividly remember the smell of incense and the sound of sacred music. Glowing colors tumbled through the stained-glass windows upon the towering Gothic arches. The whole experience was so beautiful that it was difficult *not* to pray. Beauty has the power to lift the soul to God because it is a share in the infinite beauty of the Blessed Trinity. All beauty comes from him and reflects him. As the Old Testament proclaims, "For from the greatness and beauty of created things comes a corresponding perception of their Creator" (Wisdom 13:5).

Nothing in heaven compares to the beauty of God, and nothing on earth approaches the beauty of the woman. For this reason, women have a unique role in revealing God to the world. In the words of Stasi Eldredge, "God has a beauty to unveil. A beauty that is captivating and powerfully redemptive."[30] Like God's, your beauty is powerful.

> Women have a unique role in revealing God to the world.

So the question must be asked, "How will you use your beauty?" St. John Paul II remarks that the dignity and balance of human life depend at every moment of history and in every place upon who man will be for woman and who woman will be for man.[31] So who will you be for man?

Beauty Will Save the World

The famous Russian novelist Dostoyevsky writes, "Beauty will save the world." Perhaps now more than ever—at a time when beauty is so often distorted or idolized—his statement rings true. The world needs women who understand the power of their beauty and who will use it to draw the hearts of men toward God, instead of distracting them from him. The beauty that has the greatest power is not the physical kind. In the words of Archbishop Fulton Sheen, "The beauty on the outside never gets into the soul. But the beauty of the soul reflects itself on the face."[32]

In his first letter, St. Peter writes to the Christian women, saying, "Let not yours be the outward adorning with braiding of hair, decoration of gold, and wearing of robes, but let it be the hidden person of the heart with the imperishable jewel of a gentle and quiet spirit, which in God's sight is very precious" (1 Peter 3:3-4). In saying this, he is not arguing that external beauty is bad, but rather that it must be secondary to the beauty that lasts.

His advice flies in the face of modern thought. You may have seen the silly bumper sticker that says, "Well-behaved women rarely make history." Considering that the woman most honored throughout history is the Immaculate Virgin Mary and the most revered woman of the past century was St. Teresa of Calcutta (Mother Teresa), this motto seems a bit misleading. It almost sounds defeatist, as if a woman needs to abandon virtue in favor of rebellion if she hopes to accomplish anything meaningful. The idea that a woman needs to misbehave to leave her mark is quite a disservice to women—and to the world that longs to see living models of virtue. The world needs to see the radiance, beauty, compassion, and power of true femininity.

Beauty in Action

Examples of such women can be found throughout history. In the sixteenth century the great Doctor of the Church, St. Teresa of Avila, helped reform the Church during a time of great confusion and corruption. Known especially for her mystical prayer life, she is the subject of perhaps one of the most beautiful sculptures ever crafted: Bernini's "The Ecstasy of St. Teresa." In it, the artist depicts Teresa experiencing the deepest form of mystical prayer. She does not appear somber and contemplative. Quite the opposite. As Christopher West explains:

Memorialized in stone, we see the angel of love poised to thrust his wounding arrow into Teresa's readied heart. Her face—masterfully sculpted by Bernini—tells the story of a mystic who is tasting, as John Paul describes it, "the paradoxical blending of bliss and pain" as *something akin to Jesus' experience on the Cross"* (NMI 27).[33]

In fact, Christopher West points out that "one would have to be either blind or ignorant not to notice that she looks like a bride" experiencing the bliss of nuptial union.[34] Such a description of a nun lost in prayer might seem scandalous. But we must remember that the Bible describes the one-flesh union of a husband and wife to be a great mystery as it relates to Christ and his Church (see Ephesians 5:31–32). In teaching us this, St. Paul is not implying that God's love for us is sexual, but rather that God's love for us is so intimate and fulfilling that, again, of all human experiences, the marital embrace best reflects this reality. Through this intimate union, as through the beautiful spirituality of St. Teresa, God's love for his Church becomes visible.

In the twentieth century, we also had the beautiful example of St. Teresa Benedicta of the Cross, more commonly remembered as Edith Stein. Although raised in a devout Jewish family, she considered herself an atheist as a teenager and later recalled, "I consciously and deliberately lost the habit of praying."[35]

She was gifted with an exceptional mind, and she obtained a doctorate in philosophy after being one of the first women admitted to university studies in Germany. Edith converted to the Catholic Faith upon reading the autobiography of St. Teresa of Avila and continued her academic life lecturing, teaching, writing, and translating. In her published works, she encourages women to influence society, politics, and higher education by transforming them through a woman's unique feminine gifts—or as St. John Paul II would call them, the "feminine genius."[36]

Edith Stein felt a call to the religious life and responded to this call with generosity, entering a Carmelite monastery. However, only seven years after making her final vows, she was arrested by the Nazis and executed in the gas chamber of a concentration camp. Known for her profound intellect and maternal love for others, St. Teresa Benedicta of the Cross, like St. Teresa of Avila, united a contemplative life of prayer with an active life that transformed civilization. It should also be noted that Edith Stein's essays on women influenced another European philosopher, Karol Wojtyla ... who would later become St. John Paul II.

Surveying the tremendous ways that women have been a blessing to the world, St. John Paul II writes, "To this great, immense feminine 'tradition' humanity owes a debt which can never be repaid. Yet how many women have been and continue to be valued more for their physical appearance than for their skill, their professionalism, their intellectual abilities, their deep sensitivity; in a word, the very dignity of their being!"[37]

Thank You for Being a Woman

Many who claim to dislike the Church's attitude toward women have not taken much time to read what the Church has to say about them. In his *Letter to Women,* St. John Paul II expresses deep appreciation for the unique ways that women make God present to humanity. In it, he exclaims:

Thank you, *women who are mothers!* You have sheltered human beings within yourselves in a unique experience of joy and travail. This experience makes you become God's own smile upon the newborn child, the one who guides your child's first steps, who helps it to grow, and who is the anchor as the child makes its way along the journey of life.

Thank you, *women who are wives!* You irrevocably join your future to that of your husbands, in a relationship of mutual giving, at the service of love and life.

Thank you, *women who are daughters and women who are sisters!* Into the heart of the family, and then of all society, you bring the richness of your sensitivity, your intuitiveness, your generosity and fidelity.

Thank you, *women who work!* You are present and active in every area of life—social, economic, cultural, artistic, and political. In this way you make an indispensable contribution to the growth of a culture which unites reason and feeling, to a model of life ever open to the sense of "mystery," to the establishment of economic and political structures ever more worthy of humanity.

Thank you, *consecrated women!* Following the example of the greatest of women, the Mother of Jesus Christ, the Incarnate Word, you open yourselves with obedience and fidelity to the gift of God's love. You help the Church and all mankind to experience a "spousal" relationship to God, one which magnificently expresses the fellowship which God wishes to establish with his creatures.

Thank you, *every woman,* for the simple fact of being *a woman!* Through the insight which is so much a part of your womanhood you enrich the world's understanding and help to make human relations more honest and authentic.[38]

When one reads these moving words, it becomes evident how highly St. John Paul II regarded women. If a woman feels called to be a stay-at-home mother, she is not squandering her gifts and talents. If she feels called to enter the political or academic professions, she is not displaying a lack of femininity. Rather, these areas of life require the genius of women. If a woman chooses to enter religious life, she is not rejecting motherhood. Take, for example, Sister Dierdre Byrne. She is a religious sister, a surgeon, and a colonel in the United States Army. She is not doing these things *instead* of motherhood—she is mothering *through* these things.

Later in the same letter, John Paul II recognizes that, "Women's dignity has often been unacknowledged ... This has prevented women from truly being themselves and it has resulted in a spiritual impoverishment of humanity."[39] This need not be so in the future. As John Paul II exhorts women in his letter on their dignity, *Mulieris Dignitatem* ("On the Dignity and Vocation of Women"):

> The hour is coming, in fact has come, when the vocation of women is being acknowledged in its fullness, the hour in which women acquire in the world an influence, an effect and a power never hitherto achieved. That is why, at this moment when the human race is undergoing so deep a transformation, women imbued with a spirit of the Gospel can do so much to aid humanity in not falling.[40]

The Fall of Beauty

For women to aid humanity in not falling, women must first examine the ways in which they have fallen. The book of Genesis states that with the advent of original sin, Adam and Eve's eyes were opened. However, it seems as if they saw *less* after the Fall. For example, theologians often recognize that Adam no longer saw Eve's body as an invitation to love as God loves. However, not much has been said about how Eve saw her own body after the Fall. It is reasonable to believe that she also lost the ability to see herself as God viewed her.

From the beginning of time, the devil has sought to invert and twist every truth that God wishes to communicate to us. If God wishes to say to you: "You are beautiful," the devil wants you to think, "I am not beautiful." The media will only reinforce this lie, convincing you: "I can't be beautiful because *she's* so much prettier than I am. I'm not lovely. My hips are too big, my hair is too thin, my eyes are too round, and my earlobes are uneven."

If the devil is unable to convince a woman that she is not beautiful, he will tempt her to make an idol out of her beauty and fall prey to vanity. She may then misuse her beauty for personal gain.

For example, she may flaunt her body to win emotional satisfaction at the expense of men. Just as men have wounded women through manipulation, women have at times been guilty of the same. But in the beginning, it was not so.

The Redemption of Beauty

When women are bombarded on an hourly basis with the message that they are not as beautiful as they should be, how is a woman to untwist the lie? How does she begin to heal her image of herself? The best place to start is the Word of God.

In the Song of Songs, we read about a lover who is captivated by his beloved. Throughout the history of the Church, saints have always seen this book of Scripture as a revelation of God's love for his bride, the Church. You may find it difficult to imagine, but as you read what the groom says to his bride, try to hear God himself speaking these words to you:

> Behold, you are beautiful, my love; behold, you are beautiful ... You have ravished my heart, my sister, my bride, you have ravished my heart with a glance of your eyes ... How sweet is your love, my sister, my bride! How much better is your love than wine, and the fragrance of your oils than any spice! (Song of Songs 1:15, 4:9-10).

Could you imagine God finding you so lovely and desiring you with such zeal? Why is it that most women find it so difficult to accept the fact that they are desirable, but will easily believe anything negative said about them? To heal this tendency, a woman should look to how the beloved responds to her lover in the Song of Songs. In response to his praise of her beauty, she responds:

> This is my beloved and this is my friend ... I am my beloved's and my beloved is mine ... I am my beloved's, and his desire is for me ... O that his left hand were under my head, and that his right hand embraced me! (Song of Songs 5:16, 6:3, 7:10, 8:3).

I encourage you to read this exchange between the lovers again and again, to allow God's Word into your heart.

Heaven on Earth

Not only does the Bible refer to the male-female union as a revelation of God's love for us, the Scriptures even refer to the woman's body as a foreshadowing of eternal bliss. In discussing the final coming of God and the consolation of heaven for believers, the prophet Isaiah uses the image of a child nursing at his mother's breasts:

> Rejoice with Jerusalem, and be glad for her, all you who love her; rejoice with her in joy, all you who mourn over her; that you may suck and be satisfied with her consoling breasts; that you may drink deeply with delight from the abundance of her glory (Isaiah 66:10-11).

God is not ashamed to use such imagery, because he knows there is nothing shameful in what he created. After the creation of man and woman, God looked at what he had made and declared that it was very good. In fact, there is nothing impure about the human body. As St. John Paul II says, "Purity is the glory of the human body before God. It is the glory of God in the human body, through which masculinity and femininity are manifested."[41]

In the Song of Songs, a woman's breasts are spoken of eight times, and the book is only eight chapters long. God created the body of the woman to be a visible sign of the beauty of her femininity. Her breasts reveal her unique capacity to nurture and to be a mother. Therefore, a woman's body should not be deemed impure. She might dress in a way that detracts from her dignity. The thoughts of men about her may be impure. But the body itself is very good.

> The body itself is very good.

Catholics are not the only ones to recognize this. In fact, the ancient Jewish scholar Rabbi Akiva declared, "Heaven forbid that any man in Israel ever disputed that the Song of Songs is holy. For the whole world is not worth the day on which the Song of Songs was given to Israel, for all the Writings are holy and the Song of Songs is the holy of holies."[42]

Indeed, you *are* an image of heaven on earth. If you keep this in mind, how will it impact the way you look at yourself and the way you invite men to look at you? If you appreciate your own beauty and you understand how God sees you, you will want men to look at you in the same way. In fact, you will never want to settle for a man who would view you any differently.

While you may fear that finding such a man is impossible, it is not. You have a role to play in teaching men how to look at all women. Before he became pope, Karol Wojtyla gave a presentation to college women, in which he said, "Men must be taught to love, and to love in a noble way; they must be educated in depth in this truth, that is, in the fact that a woman is a person and not simply an object."[43] The primary tool by which women educate men about their dignity is through the virtue of modesty. In the words of one woman, your mission of modesty is a "ministry of beauty."[44]

> You are an image of heaven on earth.

THE MISSION OF THE WOMAN

Edith Stein once said that young women should be "enthusiastic about the ideal of making their lives a mysterious symbol of that union which Christ contracted with his Church."[45] Upon reading this, you may think, "That's a great theological idea, but how am I, as a young woman, to apply this in my daily life?"

First, do not be afraid to open yourself to God's love. You will lose nothing of yourself by drawing near to him. In fact, the closer you get to him, the more you will become yourself. Many young women have told me, after squandering years of their lives in unhealthy relationships and estrangement

from God, "I don't even know who I am anymore." The opposite happens when we turn to him. We find our identity ... and our mission.

St. John Paul II writes, "It seems as if the specific determination of the woman, through her own body and her sex, hides what constitutes the very depth of her femininity ... the mystery of femininity manifests and reveals itself in its full depth through motherhood."[46] In other words, stamped into a woman's body is her calling to give life to others through the gift of herself in love. The form of the feminine body, according to John Paul II, is essentially maternal. He points out that the Bible, along with the Liturgy, "honors and praises throughout the centuries 'the

43

womb that bore you and the breasts from which you sucked milk' (Luke 11:27). These words are a eulogy of motherhood, of femininity, of the feminine body in its typical expression of creative love."[47] The woman's body, which has so often been degraded in the modern world and divorced from motherhood, reveals much about the essence of who God created women to be.

In virtue of being a woman, every female is called to become both bride and mother. Her body reveals this. However, not all women are called to the sacrament of Matrimony. God has blessed some women with hearts that yearn for a love that surpasses all human loves. They long to give themselves entirely to God, and so they enter the consecrated life as sisters. These women do not abandon their mission as brides and mothers by entering the religious life. Rather, they fulfill these

deep desires in a different way. Each sister becomes a bride of Christ and through her openness to his grace in her life, becomes a spiritual mother to many souls.

However, even if a woman is not called to become a consecrated sister, she is still called to holiness. Some think that all holy people are the same, but nothing could be further from the truth. It is sin that dulls our individuality. Sainthood is not about being put into a mold. That explains why every saint is so unique. Some were mild and soft-spoken, while others had, shall we say, somewhat different temperaments. When St. Teresa of Avila's carriage collapsed and she fell in the mud, she said to God, "No wonder you have so few friends, when you treat them so badly!" She could speak to God with such honesty because she had such a genuine relationship with him.

To live out what you have read in this book, begin by pursuing your own relationship with God. Better yet, allow *yourself* to be pursued by him. Like you, God is a mystery of great value who deserves to be pursued. And he will reveal himself to the one who searches in sincerity for him.

> Because you are made in the image and likeness of God, who is love, you will never find fulfillment in a relationship that does not reflect his love for you.

When it comes to human relationships, remember: Because of your great worth, do as God does. You deserve to be pursued, and there is no need to expose yourself. Rather, reveal yourself to the one man (your husband) who is worthy of your love.

Because you are made in the image and likeness of God, who is love, you will never find fulfillment in a relationship that does not reflect his love for you. Only by opening yourself to God's love will you be able to fully love another. Yet, even within a godly relationship, no human being can perfectly fulfill you. Regarding his advice to couples preparing for marriage, one priest said, "I tell them flat out that they're in for trouble if they think their marriage is going to satisfy their deepest yearning for love. Not gonna happen. Only if they set their sights on the marriage of heaven can they find the love they're looking for."[48]

There is a greater kind of love than anyone on this earth can provide. In the words of Christopher West:

> Since the dawn of creation, God has been singing to us, wooing us, enticing us, calling us, inviting us. And if we listen to the enchanting melody and unabashedly erotic lyrics of his Song, we will understand that God *longs* to "marry" us. We will understand that God's eternal plan is to espouse us to himself forever (see Hosea 2:19) so that we might share in the bliss of his own eternal Communion of love.[49]

If you respond to this invitation of love and become who you truly are as a woman, you will make visible the beautiful mystery of God's love.

PRAYERS

Heavenly Father, as your daughter, I come to you with all of my hopes and fears. You alone perfectly understand the desires of my heart and even its most hidden wounds. At times, I have turned from you, doubting your love for me. You have created me for love, but I have all too often sought to find that love apart from your plan for me. In the future, when I am tempted to run from you, please help me to trust in you. When I am tempted to settle for the kind of relationships that distract me from you, teach me how to love. When I begin to believe the world's empty idea of beauty, help me to see my body as you see it. For it is only with you that I can become who you created me to be. By your grace, may I desire nothing less. Amen.

Blessed Virgin Mary, you are a model of strength, humility, and gracefulness for all women. Because you opened your heart to God's plan, you gave Life to the world. Mary, Gate of Heaven, help me to open my heart to the grace of God, so that I can experience his love within me. Mary, Mystical Rose, teach me how to use my beauty to win souls for God. Mother of our Savior, teach me how to pray. For if I can learn to listen to the voice of God, I will know his love and reveal his beauty to the world. Amen.

NOTES

1   Alice Von Hildebrand, "Women as the Guardians of Purity," *Homiletic & Pastoral Review* (March 2004), 14-18; citation at 15.

2   *The Collegeville Bible Commentary* (Collegeville, MN: Liturgical Press, 1989), 793.

3   Dom Bernard Orchard, *A Catholic Commentary of Holy Scripture* (London: Thomas Nelson and Sons, 1953), 500.

4   Alice Von Hildebrand, *The Privilege of Being a Woman* (Ann Arbor, MI: Sapientia Press of Ave Maria University, 2005), 81-82.

5   Pope Benedict XVI, *Deus Caritas Est* 10.

6   Melinda Selmys, "The Lord God of the Living Room," *National Catholic Register,* June 10-16, 2007.

7   Christopher West, *Heaven's Song* (West Chester, PA: Ascension, 2008), 1-2.

8   Pope Benedict XVI, *Spe Salvi* 33.

9   John Paul II, *Man and Woman He Created Them: A Theology of the Body*, trans. by Michael Waldstein (Boston: Pauline, 2006), 110:7.

10 Wendy Shalit, *Girls Gone Mild* (New York: Random House, 2007), 158.

11 *Deus Caritas Est* 5.

12 Wendy Shalit, *A Return to Modesty* (New York: Touchstone, 2000), 175.

13 Alice Von Hildebrand, *The Privilege of Being a Woman*, 91.

14 Sheila Ruth, *Issues in Feminism: An Introduction to Women's Studies* (New York: McGraw-Hill, 2000).

15 Gary Ezzo and Robert Bucknam, *On Becoming Toddler Wise* (Mt. Pleasant, SC: Parent-Wise Solutions, 2003), 141.

16 Louann Brizendine, *The Female Brain* (New York: Morgan Road, 2006), 12.

17 Brizendine, 14.

18 Brizendine, 44.

[19] Brizendine, 5.

[20] E.B McClure, "A meta-analytic review of sex differences in facial expression processing and their development in infants, children, and adolescents," *Psychological Bulletin* 126:3 (May 2000): 424-453.

[21] Else-Quest, et al., "Gender differences in temperament: a meta-analysis," *Psychological Bulletin,* 132:1 (January 2006): 33-72.

[22] Brizendine, 118, 119, 123.

[23] Rosemary Ellen Guiley, *The Quotable Saint* (New York: Checkmark, 2002), 170.

[24] Dawn Eden, *The Thrill of the Chaste* (Nashville: W Publishing Group, 2006), 22.

[25] Von Hildebrand, 63.

[26] Maria Ruiz Scaperlanda, *Edith Stein* (Huntington, IN: Our Sunday Visitor, 2001), 89.

[27] L. Ali and J. Scelfo, "Choosing Virginity," *Newsweek* (December 9, 2002), 6.

[28] John and Stasi Eldredge, *Captivating* (Nashville: Nelson, 2005), 36-37.

[29] Dannah Gresh, *Secret Keeper* (Chicago: Moody, 2002), 19.

[30] Eldredge, 26.

[31] TOB 43:7.

[32] Fulton Sheen, as quoted in *True Girl* 1:1 (February/March 2006).

[33] West, 114.

[34] Ibid.

[35] As quoted in Pope Benedict XVI's "Address on the Occasion of the XX World Youth Day," Thursday, August 18, 2005.

[36] John Paul II, *Letter to Women,* June 29, 1995.

[37] Ibid.

[38] Ibid.

[39] Ibid.

[40] Second Vatican Council, *Mulieris Dignitatem,* December 8, 1965; AAS 58 (1966), 13-14.

[41] TOB 57:3.

[42] Rabbi Akiva, *Mishnah Yadayim* 3:5.

[43] Karol Wojtyla, *The Way to Christ* (San Francisco: Harper, 1982), 38.

[44] Eden, 150.

[45] Igino Giordani, "Edith Stein on the Education of Women," *L'Osservatore Romano* (March 6, 1969), 9.

[46] TOB 21:2.

[47] TOB 21:5.

[48] West, 121.

[49] West, 29.

RESOURCES

Books

How to Find Your Soulmate Without Losing Your Soul by Jason and Crystalina Evert
If You Really Loved Me by Jason Evert
Made New by Crystalina Evert
Male, Female, Other? by Jason Evert
Pure Faith by Jason Evert
Pure Love by Jason Evert
Pure Womanhood by Crystalina Evert
Saint John Paul the Great by Jason Evert
Theology of the Body in One Hour by Jason Evert

Websites

chastity.com
womenmadenew.com

ABOUT THE AUTHOR

Jason Evert earned a master's degree in theology and undergraduate degrees in counseling and theology, with a minor in philosophy, at Franciscan University of Steubenville. He is the author of more than fifteen books, including *How to Find Your Soulmate Without Losing Your Soul, The Dating Blueprint,* and *Saint John Paul the Great.* He has spoken on six continents to more than two million teens in high schools and colleges internationally, challenging young people to embrace the virtue of chastity. He runs the website Chastity.com and is the founder of Chastity Project, which is an international alliance of young people who promote chastity in more than forty countries.

THEOLOGY OF
HIS BODY

Discovering the Strength & Mission of Masculinity

JASON EVERT

ASCENSION

West Chester, Pennsylvania

Unless otherwise noted, Scripture passages are from the Revised Standard Version–Second Catholic Edition © 2006 by the Division of Christian Education of the National Council of the Churches of Christ in the United States of America. Used by permission. All rights reserved.

Scripture texts marked "NAB" in this work are taken from the New American Bible, revised edition © 2010, 1991, 1986, 1970 Confraternity of Christian Doctrine, Washington, DC, and are used by permission of the copyright owner. All rights reserved. No part of the New American Bible may be reproduced in any form without permission in writing from the copyright owner.

Ascension
PO Box 1990
West Chester, PA 19380
1-800-376-0520
ascensionpress.com

Cover design: Devin Schadt

Printed in the United States of America
24 25 26 27 28 5 4 3 2 1

ISBN 978-1-954882-45-4 (paperback)
ISBN 978-1-954882-46-1 (e-book)

CONTENTS

FOREWORD

Every man hungers to know and live the truth about life, love, and sex. The problem is that when we don't feed ourselves from the banquet of God's plan for our lives, we inevitably end up binging on junk food. Have you seen the movie *Super Size Me* about the guy who ate every meal at McDonald's for a month? Remember how he turned out? That gives us a good image of what happens to us at a deep spiritual level when we feed our hunger for love and sex from our culture's pornographic, drive-through menu.

The problem is not that we are hungry. God put that hunger for love and sex in us. It is the stuff from which great saints are made. It is also the stuff from which great sinners are made. What is the difference between the great saints and the great sinners? Where they go to feed their hunger.

You might think that you already know what the Catholic Church has to say about the issue of sexuality. You may even think it is out to starve you. However, if you read this book with an open mind, I promise you will never see things the same way again.

In a series of 129 talks, St. John Paul II demonstrates the *beauty* of God's plan for sexual love and the *joy* of living it. He called this new vision of sex, love, and the human person Theology of the Body (TOB). To say "theology of the body" is simply another way of saying "made in the image of God." This means that our bodies are not only *biological;* they are also (and even more so) *theological.* Our bodies offer us a profound "study of God," if we have the eyes to see it. Just as a work of art points to the heart of the artist, so, too, does the human body point to the heart of the God who made us.

The talks themselves are scholarly. They need to be broken open if the average reader is to benefit from them. But beyond "translating" the TOB into a language that everyone can understand, the various themes of John Paul II's talks also need to be applied to real aspects of our lives as men.

That is what you are holding in your hands right now. In *Theology of His Body* and (on the flip side) *Theology of Her Body,* Jason Evert reflects with great wit and wisdom on certain aspects of the TOB as they apply to the lives of young men and women. Through a creative application of some key principles found in the Theology of the Body, Jason helps us to reclaim the true nature and dignity of masculinity and, through that, the true nature and dignity of our humanity.

The world gives a message about the meaning of masculinity very different from the one you will find in this book. No doubt you have been told that manhood is achieved by conquering women for the sake of ourselves, but the truth is that manhood is found in conquering ourselves for the sake of others.

Through this full giving of ourselves, we discover why God has made us men. In fact, if we don't successfully answer the question "Why did God make us to be men?" we will miss out on the very purpose and meaning of our existence. So read this book with an open mind. And read it with a hungry heart. It will lead you to the banquet of love that really satisfies.

–Christopher West
Theology of the Body Institute

INTRODUCTION

When I was in high school, if someone handed me a book about the bodies of men and women, I would be far more interested in reading about her anatomy than my own. Perhaps you feel the same. In fact, it wouldn't surprise me if you have already browsed through the girls' book. If so, don't be ashamed.

There is a reason why the human body is fascinating: God made us that way. You may have been led to believe that you shouldn't feel the way you do, and that if you just become a really good and holy boy, you won't be so interested in the subject of sexuality. Not true. In fact, the closer you get to God, the more you become who he made you to be as a man. Your sexual drive will not be eliminated. It will be perfected in love.

Such a concept might sound strange because you may have always thought that sexual thoughts should be kept as far away from religious thoughts as possible. This division is not from God. After all, he is the one who created the gift of sexuality. He is the architect of the male and female human bodies.

By examining the way God designed your body—and even your desires—you can learn who you are as a man, how you should live, and who made you.

In the beginning …

We know from the book of Genesis that God created men and women "in his image and likeness." We know from the first letter of John that "God is love" (1 John 4:8). Therefore, men and women

3

are made in the image and likeness of Love. This isn't hard to see. Look at the design of the male and female bodies. They are made for each other. In fact, neither one makes complete sense apart from the other. The man's body is made for a woman's body—made to be a life-giving gift to her. *Her* body reveals *his* calling.

However, the calling of a man to make a gift of himself has been warped by original sin and often derailed by personal sin. Instead of giving, men often resort to taking. Instead of seeing the woman as a sister in humanity, he reduces her to an object of his lust. No man is free from the effects of original sin and personal sin, but God offers to us all the hope of redemption.

No matter how far we fall away from God's plan for our lives, we always bear in our own bodies a reminder of who we are called to become.

CHAPTER 1

STRENGTH TO SERVE AND SACRIFICE

On the flip side of this book, *Theology of Her Body*, I discussed how the woman's body reveals her identity. Her body reveals that she was made for relationships, that she possesses great beauty, and that she has a deep element of mystery about her.

True masculinity requires interior strength.

All of this can be seen by looking at the way God created her body. The physical traits reflect her unseen feminine qualities. Likewise, a man's body speaks volumes about what masculinity means and who he is created to be.

When one contrasts the male and female bodies, one of the most obvious differences between them is the strength of the man compared to the gracefulness of the feminine figure. Strength has always been associated with masculinity. This is one reason why professional athletes are so revered by men and women alike. Even in the movies, superheroes have chiseled, muscular physiques, while villains are sometimes portrayed as lazy and out of shape. Perhaps the only time Hollywood portrays a hero as being unfit is when the movie is a comedy. It seems laughable that a real man would lack strength.

However, the strength of the male body points to something deeper. It reveals the interior strength that men possess. This is not to say that women lack the ability and strength to endure suffering with courage. Having witnessed the births of my children, I can testify that if men were the ones who had to give birth, the world's population would plummet. Nonetheless, the physical attribute

of strength points to the deeper reality that true masculinity requires interior strength. Things like conviction, perseverance, character, and courage define a man more than anything else. In fact, how disappointing it is to find a man who can toil and sacrifice anything to have a great physique but seems incapable of resisting a single temptation.

Strength of the Soul

In 1852, a hunter by the name of Francois Dorel was passing through a small village in Ars, France. He heard that an exceptionally holy priest lived there, and he decided to hike by the parish to see why such crowds had gathered to see this supposed saint. While he was walking near the church with his hunting dog, St. John Vianney passed by him. The saint stopped, looked into his soul, and said, "It is greatly to be wished that your soul was as beautiful as your dog."

> If a man does not possess interior strength, he is a walking contradiction of what it means to be a man.

External qualities are valued by the world, but their worth is superficial. If a man does not possess interior strength, he is a walking contradiction of what it means to be a man. This is why a soldier's value is revealed only under the pressure of battle. A friend of mine who served in the Marines told me that many platoon commanders were astonished to see how some of the outspoken and physically strongest men wilted under pressure, while humble men of unimpressive stature often demonstrated astonishing courage.

A perfect example of such a man was St. John Paul II. A few years before he passed away, I had the blessing of meeting him in Rome. Following a private Mass, the Holy Father slowly walked with a cane to a chair where he could greet each person in attendance. Although he was an avid athlete and outdoorsman as a young man, the years had taken their toll on him. When I approached him, I noticed his hand trembling from Parkinson's disease as he sat hunched over in his chair. Here was a man who was orphaned as a youth, survived Nazism, contributed to the fall of communism, and was entrusted with the spiritual responsibility for more than a billion souls. As he looked into my eyes during our brief conversation, I realized that I have never met someone who possessed such strength, and therefore, masculinity. He was truly in the image of the One who created him.

God as Warrior

Have you ever noticed that the majority of people in church are women? One reason for this may be that, in recent years, some within the Church have sought to rid God of all masculine qualities. Some liturgists have sought to introduce "gender-inclusive" language and have even gone so far as to strip out any references to God as Father. "After all," they say, "we don't want to offend or exclude anyone." Many homilies reflect this trend. Rarely is God spoken of as a judge or a king who deserves honor and obedience. God is kind and merciful, but if that's all we hear about him, men won't understand the point of genuflecting. More often than not, when one goes to church, one hears songs about being sensitive to others. When God is described in this way, he sounds a lot like a Santa Claus.

Of what use is such a God to the one who cries out, "Deliver me from my enemies, O my God, protect me from those who rise up against me, deliver me from those who work evil, and save me from bloodthirsty men" (Psalm 59:1-3)? In the book of Psalms, King David announces his confidence in the Almighty: "I am not afraid of ten thousands of people who have set themselves against me round about. Arise, O Lord! Deliver me, O my God! For you strike all my enemies on the cheek, you break the teeth of the wicked" (Psalm 3:6-7).

In the book of Psalms, we also read, "If a man does not repent, God will whet his sword; he has bent and strung his bow; he has prepared his deadly weapons, making his arrows fiery shafts" (Psalm 7:12). Elsewhere, David writes:

> Oppose, LORD, those who oppose me; war upon those who make war upon me ... Rise up in my defense. Brandish lance and battle-ax against my pursuers. Say to my heart, 'I am your salvation.' Let those who seek my life be put to shame and disgrace. Let those who plot evil against me be turned back and confounded. Make them like chaff before the wind, with the angel of the LORD driving them on. Make their way slippery and dark, with the angel of the LORD pursuing them (Psalm 35:1-6, NAB).

Those who seek to emasculate God might read these passages, and say, "Battle axes and breaking teeth? Well, that's not very nice of God." Indeed, nowhere in Scripture is God described as being nice. He is a God who fights for his beloved.

In C.S. Lewis' masterpiece *The Lion, the Witch, and the Wardrobe,* a young girl expresses her apprehension about meeting Aslan the Lion (who is a symbol of Christ). Before encountering him, Lucy inquires:

"Is he—quite safe? I shall feel rather nervous about meeting a lion."

The answer she receives is a perfect description of the essence of God:

"Safe? … Who said anything about safe? 'Course he isn't safe. But he's good. He's the King, I tell you."

Ask any man who has served in the military, and he will testify that men will follow this kind of leader into oncoming fire. The same is true of spiritual warfare. An emasculated God is an impotent God. As a result, men won't take religion seriously. Spiritual matters will be left to women. Only when the full truth of God is revealed, do men and women discover who they are created to be. Likewise, when men and women live out authentic masculinity and femininity, they reveal something of God to the world.

The Man of God as Warrior

A seventeen-year-old guy once said to me, "I know it's wrong to sleep with some girl you don't care about, but what if you really love her? You see, the girl I'm with now, I would die for her. I'm serious. If someone put a gun to her head, I'd tell them to shoot me instead. That's how much I love this girl."

My response? "OK. Do it."

He looked at me with bewilderment. "Huh?"

I explained, "Die for her. Look: It's fun to imagine a scenario where you make a heroic sacrifice to save a woman's life. God put that noble desire on your heart for a reason. But let's face it: It's not going to happen. Unless your girlfriend is involved in organized crime, she's probably not going to be held up at gunpoint today. But there's someone you do need to protect her from, and that's yourself. If you really want to die for her, let your lust die. If you really want to guard her, guard her soul. In other words, if someone did shoot your girlfriend, is she prepared to meet God? Have you protected her eternal life? Or, perhaps, are you more interested in her body than her soul?"

This young man was not a heartless player. In my eyes, he represents all of us. We all desire to do what is noble and valiant. But our aspirations often become tainted. Our intentions are not always as pure as we know they ought to be. Our minds and wills—and even our hearts—need to be formed according to the truth.

The Model of Manhood

Because God became a man when he took on our human nature, this has given men a unique opportunity to see God's plan for masculinity in Jesus Christ. Hundreds of years before Christ was born, it was prophesied in the book of Isaiah that the long-awaited Messiah would be a Suffering Servant. He would sacrifice himself to save others (see Isaiah 52–53). In this, he is the model of all men. We are called to make sacrifices for the good of others and not to sacrifice others selfishly for our own good.

You could think of this as a creed for what it means to be a man. Or, in the words of the Jesuit motto that can often be found in all-boys high schools, we should be "men for others."

The opposite of the sacrificial servant is the domineering man who cares little for the well-being of others. He is self-absorbed. To free us from the slavery of such a contorted idea of masculinity, Jesus proclaimed, "The Son of man came not to be served but to serve, and to give his life as a ransom for many" (Matthew 20:28). Elsewhere in Scripture, husbands are commanded to love their wives as Christ loved the Church, offering his life for her (see Ephesians 5:25).

As my wife and I prepared for our wedding, we had to decide which Bible readings we would have during the Mass. Couples commonly use the wedding feast at Cana or a passage about loving each other. Therefore, Crystalina was a bit surprised when I asked whether she minded if we used the crucifixion passages for our Gospel reading. To many of the people in attendance at our wedding Mass, I suppose it was a bit strange. What they saw was a young couple pledging their love to each other. What they heard was the account of a man who was beaten, stripped, scourged, and murdered.

But to me, it said everything about the promise I was about to make to my bride. In the words of Jesus himself, "Greater love has no man than this, that a man lay down his life for his friends" (John 15:13). In giving his body for his bride, he gave her life. By no means have I perfected what I promised, but I can always return to the crucifix to see the model of how I ought to love my bride.

Not long ago, I heard of another young husband who integrated the witness of Christ into his wedding. During the wedding reception, he and his wife veered from the common tradition where the groom pulls off his bride's garter (a narrow band of fabric above her knee) and tosses it to a rowdy mob of single men. Instead of repeating this useless custom, he had his bride sit on a chair as he knelt before her and washed her feet in front of everyone. In the same way, Jesus washed the

We are called to make sacrifices for the good of others, and not to sacrifice others selfishly for our own good.

feet of his disciples before he offered his life for them on the Cross (see John 13:1-15). By imitating the humility of Christ in the sight of his wedding guests, this groom left each of them with an icon of love that they would not soon forget. But he wasn't putting on a show for his guests. He was showing them how his new wife deserved to be loved.

The Fall of Strength

Unfortunately, we do not always succeed in loving women as they ought to be loved. Not long ago, a man emailed me to ask for prayers for the soul of a young woman who had just passed away. "Jessica," as I'll call her, had been involved in prostitution and perhaps porn and suffered a stroke while on drugs. She fell into a coma and died, leaving behind a six-year-old daughter of an unknown father. Her family friend sent me a lengthy email, mourning the fact that so many guys lust after women on the Internet, without even knowing whether the model is dead or alive. The sheer morbidity of lusting after a deceased woman should make any man realize the emptiness of lust. He wrote, "Instead of admiring the acts that the women are performing … pray for them."

When one reads the tragic life of Jessica, it is obvious that she made some bad decisions. However, a serious question arises: Where were the men in her life? John Paul II said that the dignity and balance of human life depends at every moment of history and in every place on the globe upon who man will be for woman, and who woman will be for man.[1] Who had Jessica become for men, and who had they become for her?

Predators or Protectors?

The men in her life did not make sacrifices for her or use their strength to serve her. Rather, they had become exploiters. She was sacrificed on the altar of their lust. The man who cooperated with Jessica in creating the gift of life refused to give their child the gift of his fatherhood. The men who used her in prostitution, as the saying goes, were not paying her for sex. They were paying her to leave afterward. She had also fallen into the habit of using men for her own profit. She had taken the gift of beauty that God had given her and used it to ensnare men into a life of sin.

Some may read her story and assume, "Well, I'm not like *those* guys. I don't abandon women or use prostitutes. I'm a pretty good guy." However, Christ challenges each of us, "You have heard that it was said, 'You shall not commit adultery.' But I say to you that every one who looks at a woman lustfully has already committed adultery with her in his heart" (Matthew 5:27-28). To many, the command of Christ to purify every hidden corner of our imagination may seem like an impossible request. Some may question, "Considering the way women dress today and the sexual images that bombard every man through the media, does Christ really understand what he is asking of us?" Indeed, he does. But he would never command us to live a certain way without giving us every grace to fulfill the calling.

> "But I say to you that everyone who looks at a woman lustfully has already committed adultery with her in his heart" (Matthew 5:27–28).

The Redemption of Strength

One of the greatest obstacles to purity in the modern world is the mistaken notion that sexual desire is the same thing as lust (which is the reduction of another person to their sexual value). In fact, many people consider the terms "sexual" and "sinful" to be practically synonymous. For a Christian man, such a mentality is enough to cause him to become neurotic. He may think, "How am I—with all of my desires toward women—supposed to become pure if having those desires is impure? I only have two options. I can either repress all of my passions to make God happy, or I can indulge in my lust and make myself happy."

What this man doesn't realize is that repression is not pleasing to God, and indulgence will not satisfy any man. Thankfully, these are not the only two ways to react to the sexual urge.

In his book *Man and Woman He Created Them: A Theology of the Body*, St. John Paul II speaks about the redemption of our bodies. A redemption is when something is bought back or painstakingly restored to its original purpose. Therefore, the pope is calling us to rediscover the original meaning of our bodies. In the beginning, when Adam first saw Eve, they were still in a state of innocence. St. John Paul II points out: "On seeing the woman created by God, man's first words express wonder and admiration, or even better, the sense of fascination (cf. Genesis 2:23)."[2] In the beginning, Adam experienced the sexual urge as a pure desire. Although Adam was captivated by the female form, he did not see Eve as a thing to be used or conquered for his gratification. Rather, he saw in her body

the invitation to love her in a way that would make visible the love of God—a love that is free, total, faithful, and life-giving. However, due to original sin, our ability to see this invitation to love has been tainted.

The Battlefield

To paraphrase St. John Paul II, our hearts have become a battlefield between love and lust. The more lust dominates our hearts, the less we experience the "spousal meaning of the body."[3] What he means about the "spousal meaning of the body" is that the bodies of men and women reveal that they are made for one another.

They have been created to become a gift to each other. This is so unmistakable that it is stamped into their anatomy. However, we no longer see clearly. When a man gazes upon a woman's body, does he see his invitation to truly love her, or is he immediately tempted to use her? Does he see her as a reflection of heaven or a distraction from it? His problem is not the beauty of the woman's body. His problem is that he must re-learn how to look at her—and not merely "look" at her but *see* her as God created her to be. As John Paul II says, Christ "assigns the dignity of every woman as a task to every man."[4]

One way to do this is to reflect upon the love between the bride and groom in the Song of Songs. In it, the lover refers to the woman as "my sister, my bride" (Song of Songs 4:9). Such an expression probably strikes you as a bit awkward, since no one associates romantic language with one's sister. However, the reason why the lover in the Song of Songs can love his bride fully is because he first sees her as a sister in humanity. Brothers want what's best for their sisters. They guard them against those whose motives are not pure.

If the groom in the Song of Songs did not possess this brotherly affection, how could he truly love her? As Christopher West points out, "Left to itself in this fallen world, the mere sexual urge would not recognize the woman as 'sister.' And for lack of such recognition, it could not recognize her properly as 'bride.' She would be for him only an object of appropriation—that is, an object to be grasped, possessed, used."[5]

When a man looks at a woman as a sister, it causes him to examine his own identity and mission. In the words of St. John Paul II, "The 'sister' in some sense helps the man to define and conceive himself, she becomes, I would say, a challenge in this direction."[6] It calls each man to recognize his role as a brother toward her. Such a transformation of motives demands interior strength. However, this does not spoil a man's ability to love the woman. It saves it.

If you hope to love a woman as God intended her to be loved, always remember that the terms "sister" and "bride" can never be fragmented. Even though marriage may be a decade away for you, know that now is the time for you to train yourself as a groom. Even if you feel called to the priesthood instead of marriage, you must still know how to love women properly. Therefore, now is the time to learn to love women as sisters.

Patient Transformation

Purity is not a matter of wrestling our lust to the ground and putting it into a submission hold. Ultimately, it is about allowing God to transform our hearts so that we desire the good of others. It is about asking him with sincerity to transform our hearts so that we see the true mystery and dignity of woman revealed through her body. It is an increase in love. As St. John Paul II teaches, "Love is confident in the victory of good and is ready to do everything in order that good may conquer."[7]

If you ask God with sincerity in your heart, "God, help me to love women properly," he will give you the grace to do so. Your heart will change, so that you will be motivated to love women not simply as an act of obedience to God or to do the moral thing, but truly from your heart. This transformation of the will takes time, patience, and prayer. Relearning how to look at women is not merely a decision. It is a process. It involves a massive transformation of one's heart. But it is only through dying to ourselves that we will become men.

Through this renovation of our hearts, minds, and wills, we begin to experience a greater interior freedom. The sexual urge—instead of being seen as the problem—begins to illuminate the solution. Purity of heart becomes the lens by which we can see the revelation of God in the body. To the degree that a man's heart is redeemed, the woman's body reveals to him his call to love, and he no longer sees her body as a mere temptation to lust. Our erotic desires (*eros* in Greek) may be in need of inner transformation, but they are *not* evil in themselves. In the words of St. John Paul II, this inner change allows man to experience "that fullness of 'eros,' which implies the upward impulse of the human spirit toward what is true, good and beautiful, so that what is 'erotic' also becomes true, good, and beautiful."[8]

What he is saying may sound too good to be true, but it is possible.

> Our erotic desires (eros in Greek) may be in need of inner transformation, but they are *not* evil in themselves.

In his first letter to the Church, Pope Benedict XVI notes that some accuse Christianity of poisoning *eros.* He rhetorically asks, "Doesn't the Church, with all her commandments and prohibitions, turn to bitterness the most precious thing in life? Doesn't she blow the whistle just when the joy which is the Creator's gift offers us a happiness which is itself a certain foretaste of the Divine?"[9] On the contrary, he answers, "*Eros* needs to be disciplined and purified if it is to provide not just fleeting pleasure, but a certain foretaste of the pinnacle of our existence, of that beatitude for which our whole being yearns."[10]

It is only through purification and discipline that a man will experience the fullness of what erotic love is intended to be. In the words of Christopher West, "Purity doesn't annihilate erotic desire, it perfects it."[11]

The Perfection of Love

The perfection of a man's sexual desires requires that he use his interior strength to serve and sacrifice. When he is tempted to look at a woman as an object of lust, he calls to mind that her body reveals his call to love her. When tempted to become a slave to his weakness, he calls to mind the strength God has given him. When tempted to use her, he recalls that he must love her as a sister. Doing so will enable him to love her appropriately as a bride. By loving women in this way, men make visible the love of God, who gave his life for his bride, the Church.

These ideas form a tremendous challenge for every man. However, we are worthy of such a challenge. St. John Paul II once remarked that "Young people are always searching for the beauty in love. They want their love to be beautiful. If they give in to weakness, following [worldly] models of behavior ... in the depths of their hearts they still desire a beautiful and pure love. This is as true of boys as it is of girls. Ultimately, they know that only God can give them this love. As a result, they are willing to follow Christ, without caring about the sacrifices this may entail."[12]

> The perfection of a man's sexual desires requires that he use his interior strength to serve and sacrifice.

CHAPTER 2

GOD INITIATES THE GIFT OF LOVE

Imagine you were dating a young woman who invited you to a picnic on the beach at sunset. After dinner, she begins telling you how much you mean to her and how she wants to spend the rest of her life with you. Looking deep into your eyes, she reaches into her purse and pulls out a small jewelry box. Falling down on one knee, she opens it up and asks you to be her groom.

Regardless of how you feel for her, the experience would probably be disturbing and awkward. But why? Why is it your job to ask her? If everyone today claims to be in favor of equality between the sexes, why is it romantic for a man to propose on bended knee, while a woman doing the same looks desperate? Some may claim that this is all due to social conditioning, but I would argue that there is something much deeper going on.

The man initiates the gift of love because he is the man, not because of what society has told him to do. Initiating love is not what he *ought* to do, it is part of who he *is*. It becomes easier to understand this when we remember that a person's body reveals deep mysteries about who that person is.

The Divine Plan for Human Love

In terms of sexuality, when one considers the anatomy of a man, it is obvious that he is the one who initiates the gift of himself to the woman. She is the one who receives him. Her role is not a passive one, but rather one that is actively receptive. In the Song of Songs, which is an erotic love poem at the very center of the Bible, we read of the exchange between the lover and the woman he pursues as his bride.

Groom: "I come to my garden, my sister, my bride ..."

Bride: "I slept, but my heart was awake. Hark! my beloved is knocking."

Groom: "Open to me, my sister, my love, my dove, my perfect one ..."

Bride: "My beloved put his hand to the latch, and my heart was thrilled within me. I arose to open to my beloved" (Song of Songs 5:1-2, 4-5).

The groom does not knock the door down or manipulate her to open it. Rather, he approaches her with reverence, referring to her as "my garden, my sister, my bride ... my love, my dove, my perfect one." She knows his motives are true, and she receives him willingly. But you will notice that his desire for her is not merely one of disinterested friendship. He is captivated by her. He says elsewhere, "You have ravished my heart, my sister, my bride, you have ravished my heart with a glance of your eyes" (Song of Songs 4:9). He praises the beauty of her body, including her neck, her breasts, her mouth, her face, and even her voice and her scent. He then adds, "You are all fair, my love; there is no flaw in you" (Song of Songs 4:7).

Some may read this and wonder why God would put such imagery in the Bible. We shouldn't be astonished. God is the one who blessed women with such beauty. God is the one who created us male and female and declared that it was "very good" (Genesis 1:31).

Through the union of a man and a woman, God makes visible his love for mankind and his plan to be eternally united with us in heaven. This may seem shocking to some, but Christ repeatedly referred to himself as the Bridegroom. St. Paul exclaimed that the one-flesh union of a husband and wife is a great mystery as it relates to Christ and his Church (see Ephesians 5:31-32). In teaching us this, the Bible is not implying that God's love for us is sexual, but rather it is telling us how intimate and fulfilling God's love for us is. All human analogies to describe the love between God and man are inadequate, but St. John Paul II contended that the spousal analogy is the least inadequate. In other words, he said, it is the best analogy we humans can find to describe the bliss of eternal union with God.

Heaven on Earth

Have you ever wondered why men are so often captivated by women, or why they have such a deep yearning to be united with what is beautiful? Have you ever felt like asking God, "Why did you give me all of these desires?" God placed those desires within you for a reason.

In the Old Testament, God speaks to the prophet Ezekiel and refers to his wife as "the delight of your eyes" (Ezekiel 24:16). Immediately after, the Lord speaks to Israel, referring to God's sanctuary as "the delight of your eyes, and the desire of your soul" (Ezekiel 24:21). For Jews, their earthly sanctuary was supposed to reflect heaven itself, where God dwells. If this is the case, then God has revealed that women are an earthly reflection of the paradise of heaven. When we behold the face of God in heaven, we will realize that he is the ultimate delight of our eyes and the deepest desire of our souls. Until that day comes, women foreshadow the beauty of heaven itself. No wonder we find them so fascinating.

> Women foreshadow the beauty of heaven itself. No wonder we find them so fascinating.

Commenting on the Song of Songs, Christopher West notes:

The longing of the lover for "pure beauty" is both an echo of "the beginning" and a premonition of the future. In the beginning, before sin, the naked human body perfectly reflected the beauty of God. That beauty was lost because of the "blemish" and "stain" of original sin. But at the end of time, the bodies of all who respond to the divine marriage proposal will be raised to a level of participation in God's beauty beyond even that of the beginning. The lover of the Song yearns for this, as do we all.[13]

Therefore, when you see a beautiful woman, do not be afraid of the way your entire being might respond to her. It has been said that when a man sees an attractive woman, in about a third of a second, chemical reactions erupt in his brain, sending hormones surging through his bloodstream, dilating his pupils, flushing his skin, increasing his heart rate, and changing his muscle tone. If woman are an echo of Eden and a foreshadowing of heaven, it is not surprising that God endowed them with such an ability to captivate us. God is simply trying to get our attention.

Therefore, never be shamed into thinking that you are bad for having strong sexual desires. This is part of who God created you to be as a man. Your testosterone level is about twenty times higher than girls your age, and therefore your desires will be much more intense.[14] The area of your brain dedicated to the sexual drive is also twice as large as a woman's.[15] Despite what some girls may lead you to believe, this is not a defect in you. However, your task as a man is to order these desires according to the demands of authentic love.

Pursue Her with Sincerity

The book of Tobit in the Old Testament offers us a glimpse of how to love a woman with an undivided heart. In it, we read how the archangel Raphael brought together a young couple, Tobias

> Never be shamed into thinking that you are bad for having strong sexual desires. This is part of who God created you to be as a man.

and Sarah. Although Sarah was described as "sensible, brave, and very beautiful," Tobias expressed some hesitation about marrying her. He remarked to the angel, "I have heard that the girl has been given to seven husbands and that each died in the bridal chamber ... I am afraid that if I go in I will die as those before me did, for a demon is in love with her, and he harms no one except those who approach her" (Tobit 6:13-14).

Raphael answers,

> Now listen to me, brother, for she will become your wife; and do not worry about the demon, for this very night she will be given to you in marriage ... And when you approach her, rise up, both of you, and cry out to the merciful God, and he will save you and have mercy on you. Do not be afraid, for she was destined for you from eternity. You will save her, and she will go with you, and I suppose that you will have children by her.

The book of Tobit adds, "When Tobias heard these things, he fell in love with her and yearned deeply for her" (Tobit 6:17). Another translation reads that Tobit loved Sarah "to the point of no longer being able to draw his heart away from her."[16]

On the night of their wedding, the couple joined in prayer before consummating their union. Tobias asked God's blessing upon them, saying, "'And now, O Lord, I am not taking this sister of mine because of lust, but with sincerity. Grant that I may find mercy and may grow old together with her'" (Tobit 8:7). Together, they said "Amen" and went to sleep for the night.

Upon hearing her husband utter this prayer, one can imagine that Sarah felt a deep sense of peace. As opposed to the agitation and unrest often felt by the lustful couple, there is a deep serenity that comes from living in the will of God. In the Song of Songs, the bride remarks, "I was in his eyes as one who brings peace" (Song of Songs 8:10). A woman knows the difference between being looked upon as an object and being viewed as a daughter of God. St. John Paul II considered this *the peace of the interior gaze.*[17] For Sarah, as the bride in the Song of Songs, she knew the intentions of her groom and how he looked at her.

Women are perceptive about how they are viewed. The female brain has an acute ability to read faces, judge motives, and detect nuances of speech. Some scientists theorize that this may be nature's way of equipping women with the ability to select suitable mates. Women are intellectually wired to protect themselves from men who will not protect them.

Although Tobias "yearned deeply" for this beautiful bride, he pursued her with sincerity and not because of lust. This says everything about God's plan for a man's sexuality. He does not intend to wipe out our masculinity or extinguish our passions. When a man truly loves a woman, it does not mean that he ceases to be fascinated by her or that he lacks sexual desire. Rather, he integrates the desire for her with the desire to do what is best for her. In other words, he unites *eros* (desire) and *agape* (sacrificial love).

Unfortunately, the modern world would have men and women believe that such integration is impossible. Look at modern television sitcoms. How often are men portrayed as mindless womanizers? Christian men owe it to women—and to each other—to disprove this stereotype. As St. Josemaria Escriva said, "There is need for a crusade of manliness and purity to counteract and nullify the savage work of those who think man is a beast. And that crusade is *your* work."[18]

Pursue Her

It was about ten o'clock at night during my junior year in high school when my friends and I got home from a night out. As we passed through the kitchen to load up on free food, we all gave my mom a polite "hello" as she ended a conversation on the phone. "Who was that?" I asked. "Oh, it was

Andrea's mom. Andrea is really upset and crying." With the sympathetic tenderness of a sixteen-year-old guy, I blurted, "What's her problem?" My mom replied, "Nobody asked her to the dance tonight." Our response? "Oh, there was a dance?"

With that, we all shrugged our shoulders and went into the backyard to play some basketball. Meanwhile, some cute girl on the other side of town was having huge self-esteem problems, when in reality she had nothing to worry about. We were just clueless.

To pursue women with sincerity, we also need the courage to pursue them. During college, I heard a homily that I will never forget. From the pulpit, the priest asked, "Ladies, I want you to raise your hand if you were asked out on a date this week." As would be the case on every campus in America, a meager portion of the women put their hands up. The priest then chided the men for failing to initiate relationships … and we actually appreciated it. While men are routinely criticized for failing to be gentlemen, we are rarely given concrete guidelines about how a man is supposed to act.

One way to do this is to initiate interest in a woman. Historically, it has been up to the guy to ask out the girl. The rationale behind this tradition is to honor the woman. For one, it takes the fear of rejection off the girl and places it on the guy. Second, it provides the girl with clarity, so that she doesn't have to wonder what he is thinking. Third, hopefully she will find the man's interest in her to be a compliment (provided it is expressed in an honorable way).

One reason God has given men such strong desires toward women is because we ought to pursue them. Consider, though, how this reflects the truth about God and man. The desires of men, generally speaking, are stronger than those of women. In the same way, God's desire to unite with us is stronger than our longing for him. God is the one who pursues a relationship with us, and it is he who proposes his love to us. He is the one who offers his body for his bride, that she may have life through him. In the words of Scripture, "He first loved us" (1 John 4:19).

Unfortunately, we often reject his proposal.

The Fall of the Bridegroom: "Getting Some" or Giving All?

In being made in God's image and likeness, men are called in a unique way to initiate the gift of love and to pursue women with sincerity. However, if we are honest with ourselves, we know how often we fail in this mission. We fail to live according to the truth about ourselves.

In contrast to Tobias, who pursued his bride with sincerity, some men pursue women purely for lustful gratification. In the most extreme case, we see this in the crime of rape. More commonly, certain men classify themselves as "players" and boast of their sexual conquests. However, the most common tendency within all of us is the habit of subtle manipulation.

If the woman's body is considered in the Song of Songs to be an enclosed or locked garden, she alone has the freedom to entrust a man with the key. In the words of St. John Paul II, she is the "master of her own mystery." However, this is where the moral dilemma is difficult for countless men. We don't want to *force* a woman into doing something, but we have indirect ways of *enticing* her to hand over the keys. We don't want to break the door down, but we would sure like to convince her to open it.

Consider the ways in which a man might manipulate a woman toward lust. Sometimes he attempts to make a woman feel guilty if she does not satisfy his desires. Other times, he attempts to seduce her with thoughtful gestures, hoping that she will respond to him in a physical way. Or he initiates physical affection with the hope that she will want to share his desire ... or at least give in to it. All of this is not to say that women are simply victims. Women play games as well and have used and manipulated men for social, emotional, or physical gratification. We have wounded them, and they have wounded us. But in their hearts and ours, we know that we have been created for a better kind of love.

Afraid to Give?

While some men struggle with being too aggressive or manipulative in their dealings with women, many others fall into the opposite category. They become passive toward women. Some may fear rejection, so they never initiate relationships. Others are so wrapped up in the habit of pornography that they don't know how to properly relate to women. According to one husband, some turn to porn because "the woman on the screen never says 'no.'" Still others fear commitment. They don't want to give, and so they find consolation through a life of indecision. In their hearts is a nagging worry: "What if I commit and am not content? What if someone better comes along?" This phobia paralyzes many men, but you will notice that the fear is based upon one concern: themselves.

This fear is not only present in human relationships. It often reflects a lack of willingness to give oneself to God. A young man preparing for the priesthood could share the same apprehension as a man preparing to marry. Commitment requires a total gift of self, and this does not come naturally for us.

While speaking to college men, St. John Paul II noted, "We are quite ready to take, or conquer, in terms of enjoyment, profit, gain, and success—and even in the moral order. Then comes the question of giving, and at this point we hang back, because we are not prepared to give. The element which is so characteristic under other forms in the spiritual portrait of women [that is, giving oneself] is barely perceptible in men."[19]

> Commitment requires a total gift of self, and this does not come naturally for us.

When a man enters a dating relationship, a marriage, or even the priesthood, he is being called to reject passivity. For example, boyfriends will often pat themselves on the back if they say to their girlfriends, "I don't want to pressure you to do anything that you're not ready for." Implied in this statement, however, is the assumption that the guy is willing to take all that she will give. He feels like a gentleman because he is not forcing her to do anything, yet he has become morally and spiritually limp. His character is passive, and he has no deep convictions about the value of her soul or his. The same could be said of a husband who fails to spiritually lead his family or a priest who is afraid to speak the truth with conviction. If we are to become the men God has created us to be, we cannot afford to be passive.

Homosexuality

While reading this book, those who experience same-sex attraction may wonder what all this theology has to do with them. They may think, "I don't have all these 'God-given' desires to be with a woman. I enjoy being friends with girls and I can recognize a beautiful woman when I see one, but my desires aren't for them." Such individuals often presume that their very existence is a disappointment to God. One even told me that always felt like a "walking abomination" because of the attractions he felt for other guys. This burden was finally lifted when he discovered what the Church actually teaches about the subject.

Imagine how difficult it would be to believe in the existence of an all-loving God if he condemned people for having attractions that they never chose in the first place! Although we choose what we do with our attractions—and those choices have a moral value—we do not choose to feel those desires. Therefore, because it is not a sin to feel an attraction, our holiness is not measured by who we find attractive. If it were, we would all be in trouble! If you think about it, the vast majority of sexual attractions we experience in life are not moral to act upon. Because every person experiences the effects of original sin, our inclinations don't always point us to what is good.

Original sin causes us all to have darkened intellects, weakened wills, and disordered desires. An example of a man with a darkened intellect could be the husband who sees nothing wrong with looking at porn, as long as he doesn't physically cheat on his wife. An example of a weakened will could be the guy who feels unable to resist even the smallest temptations. An example of a disordered desire would be the man who craves sexual experiences that humiliate or degrade others. In each case, original sin is manifested in a different way.

Upon hearing this, some may think, "That's terrible. Is the Church really telling everyone that their desires are disordered?" Yes. If the Church remained silent on the issue, it would be as unforgivable as a doctor who didn't want to offend his patient by speaking the truth about the results of his X-ray. Could you imagine if a hospital were sued for hate speech because they insisted that their patients were ill? Those who attacked the hospital for such intolerance would actually be harming the patients by telling them that there is no need for healing.

If every person—regardless of their attractions—experiences desires that are disordered, how can we know which ones are rightly ordered? To do this, we must consider God's plan for human sexuality. Although he did create it for pleasure and to foster emotional bonding, it is also ordered towards procreation. To divorce reproduction from sexuality would be like divorcing digestion from eating. One exists for the other, and it is neither healthy nor natural to separate the two. This is why masturbation and contraception, as well as sexual acts between members of the same sex contradict God's plan for sexuality.

The origin of same-sex attraction is not easy to explain, and the subject is fiercely debated. Some men say that they never could relate to masculinity because their fathers were emotionally unavailable to them. Others state that they were never able to fit in with their male peers. To fill the void, they yearn for masculine love and acceptance in a drastic way. Others bear wounds of sexual abuse, and they trace their sexual desires to those early memories. Many experienced none of these things, and cannot explain the origin of their attractions. All they know is that these feelings have been present for as long as they can remember.

But no matter what a person's attractions are, where they came from, how intense they are, or how permanent or transitory they might be, they do not define a person's identity. First and foremost, men who experience homosexual attractions are beloved sons of God and should not be treated as second-class citizens in the Church. Like all their brothers in Christ, they are called to grow in self-mastery, practice the virtue of chastity, and pursue a life of holiness.

The effects of original sin impact every man and take their toll on every human relationship. However, there is no wound, addiction, or vice that is beyond the power of Christ's redemption. You may struggle with believing that such conversion of heart is possible. You may fear what it will cost you. Christ alone gives the answers to your questions about life and love. But as John Paul II has said, "Even if they are demanding answers, the young are not afraid of them; more to the point, they even await them."[20]

The Redemption of the Bridegroom

Being made in the image and likeness of God, a man receives his marching orders in his own body. The sight of a man's body reveals that he has not been made for himself. He has been created to make a gift of himself to others. This is precisely why a passive, fearful, or self-absorbed man does not reflect God's nature. Such a man does not even reflect his own nature.

Speaking of the first man created by God, one woman remarked: "Adam is captured best in motion, doing something. His essence is strength in action. That is what he speaks to the world. He bears the image of God, who is a warrior. On behalf of God, Adam says, 'God will come through. God is on the move.' That is why a passive man is so disturbing. His passivity defies his very essence. It violates the way he bears God's image. A passive man says, 'God will not come through. He is not acting on your behalf.'"[21]

If we are to become who God has called us to be, we must put aside the tendency to fear and the inclination to think first of ourselves. We should not be afraid to initiate relationships, initiate dates, and

The sight of a man's body reveals that he has not been made for himself. He has been created to make a gift of himself to others.

initiate the practice of virtue within them. When it comes to expressions of physical affection, Christ calls us to examine not simply our actions, but even our motives. Instead of operating under the subtly self-seeking motto, "I won't force you to do anything you don't want to do," we should think, "I want her to value her purity because I value my own."

Such a change of heart is not easy. It requires deep conversion of heart. But do not fear the challenge. Your strongest temptations and desires are not meant to drive you away from God. Rather, they can be redeemed and used to unite you with him. In fact, *the yearning within your body to unite with beauty is a reminder that your soul longs for the beauty of heaven.* We all desire perfect beauty, but this longing can ultimately be fulfilled only in God. Because women radiate beauty more than anything on earth, men often look for ultimate fulfillment in them, substituting the eternal reality of heavenly bliss for its earthly reflection. In the words of one author, "The young man who rings the bell at the brothel is unconsciously looking for God."[22]

Our desires are not the problem. We must, however, allow God to transform our wills and even our hearts. If we have the courage to do this, our desires will propel us to heaven. Then, by initiating the gift of love in sincerity, we can make visible on earth the invisible love of God, who first loved us.

CHAPTER 3

GOD INITIATES THE GIFT OF LIFE

"Thanks for the chastity talk, man," a high school junior said to me. "I seriously needed it. I'm going to sign one of those chastity commitment cards because I really need to start over." He expressed his gratitude and went home with a new conviction to treat girls differently. When he arrived, he noticed a missed call on his phone. He took off his backpack, began unpacking his things, and listened to the voicemail: "Uh, Darren, this is Rachel. We got together last month at the party. Well. Um. I kinda missed my period, so I took a pregnancy test ... Um. I really need you to call me.' [*Click.*]" Darren felt sick to his stomach with fear. Rachel was some girl he hooked up with after having a few drinks at a friend's house. He hardly knew her.

Two years later, I bumped into Darren at a youth conference. His son was now over a year old, and Darren had become a wonderful dad. He never dated Rachel and added, "She's into some bad things and is still hanging out with the wrong people. But she lets me spend a lot of time with the baby, and I'm glad I get to see him so much. I got this job after school so that I can pay for all his food and stuff."

Love Is Responsibility

Although Darren didn't plan to have a child, he did choose to become a father. In an address to college men before he became pope, John Paul II spoke about the tendency to run from such a challenge. Speaking of the man who is tempted to reject the demands of fatherhood, he said, "When he takes his pleasure, he must also take his responsibility." He added that when life is conceived, "a frightening moral danger begins," because the man can fall into the role of an exploiter. This tendency will control a man "if he does not make use of his own interior strength—the strength of his intellect and his will and even his heart—in order to mature into the role of father."[23]

If it is the male task to initiate the gift of life, a young man must choose wisely when and through whom he will bring life into the world. Think deeply about this: By abstaining from sex until he is married, a young man is actually doing what is best for his future children by not conceiving them yet. He knows that now is not the time for him to become a father. So he sacrifices his desires for the good of others. He postpones gratification. He abstains.

Instead of abstaining, some choose to gamble with the futures of others. They disregard the wisdom of waiting and indulge their sexual urges at the expense of women and children. They cross their fingers, hoping that they won't "accidentally" impregnate anyone. Although they claim to be confident, they live in fear. Instead of seeing their fertility as a gift, it is viewed as an inconvenient obstacle that complicates their quest for pleasure. Should pregnancy occur, such men often think that something went wrong. They say, "How could this have happened?" It seems that such a man is afraid of how he was created. If we are living as we ought, we have nothing to fear. As Scripture tells us, "There is no fear in love, but perfect love casts out fear. For fear has to do with punishment, and he who fears is not perfected in love" (1 John 4:18).

Therefore, follow the advice of Proverbs 24:27, which reads, "Prepare your work outside, get everything ready for you in the field; and after that build your house." We should not engage in the act that creates a family until we are prepared to bear the responsibility for one.

You may be thinking that the demands of fatherhood are still many years away from you. And if you're in high school, hopefully this will be the case. However, St. John Paul II said that young men should begin to assume gradual responsibility for it. One way to do this is to accept and be grateful for your ability to create life. In John Paul II's own words, "God who is Father, who is Creator, planted a reflection of his creative strength and power within man … We should sing hymns of praise to God the Creator for this reflection of himself in us—and not only in our souls but also in our bodies."[24]

The very nature of God's creative love is stamped into our male anatomy. This is one way we reflect the image and likeness of God in our masculinity; we initiate the gift of life. The woman does not. Rather, she receives it. Thus, the Scriptures do not call God our mother. God does not receive life from anyone. He is the Author of life. This fact doesn't make men greater than women, because men and women are both made in his image and likeness. Men initiate the gift, but the woman's body becomes a tabernacle of life. The miracle of conception occurs within her.[25]

The Supreme Gift

While golfing with a friend, I struck up a conversation with one of the men we were paired with. I asked him if he was married and had any kids. Without hesitation, he replied, "No way, man. Kids scare me to death."

I do not remember the last time I felt so sorry for an individual. So, before we hit our next shot, I gave him an uplifting thought about growing old and lying alone on his deathbed because he was too afraid of having kids.

The reason for my not-so-subtle guilt trip is because I didn't want him to miss out on the greatest joy a man can experience this side of heaven. In my own experience, nothing on earth is greater than fatherhood. Pleasure, wealth, achievements, and success may be satisfying, but they are incapable of fulfilling us. Fatherhood, on the other hand, is eternal. In the words of the Church, "Children are really the supreme gift of marriage."[26]

One of my high school teachers was a young married man whose eyes would tear up whenever he spoke about his children. I was sixteen at the time, and I remember thinking that he seemed a bit overly attached to them. Now that I'm a father, I know what he felt and can testify that it is something that cannot be explained—only experienced. Therefore, do not be afraid of fatherhood. It would be more sensible to fear winning the lottery.

The calling of fatherhood is stamped into our own bodies!

All Men Are Called to Fatherhood

The mission of being a father is something that every man is called to do. It is stamped into our bodies. However, fatherhood can be lived out in many ways. Husbands fulfill the call to fatherhood in one way, and priests fulfill this call in another way. The reason we call priests "Father" is because they also lay down their lives in sacrifice to unite themselves with their bride—the Church. Like husbands, priests freely commit to making a total and faithful gift of themselves. In doing so, they give spiritual life to others. Their God-given desire to become fathers is fulfilled because they participate in the generation of life—eternal life.

Some guys imagine that God is not calling them to the priesthood because they want to be dads. However, what type of priest would a man be if he had no desire to give life to others? Life-giving love is the essence of the priesthood, in imitation of Christ.

Even those who do not feel called to the priesthood or married life are still called to become fathers in their own way. It is inevitable that their younger classmates, nephews and nieces, neighbors, and siblings will look to them as a model of how a man should live. By becoming the man God wants them to be, they will play a fatherly role in the development of others. For example, on my college campus, some guys participated in a program for underprivileged kids from broken families. They would spend time with the children each week, playing basketball or helping them with homework. For many of the kids, these selfless college men were the closest thing to a father figure that they would ever experience. Thank God that he stamped this calling into our bodies, lest we forget the great mission he has entrusted us with—to give life to others.

The Fall of Fatherhood

When a man rejects the mission of fatherhood, untold suffering often results. During the summer before my first year in high school, I sat in silence as I watched my best friend repeatedly stab an expensive painting his father had given him with a screwdriver. Each time he punctured the canvas with his tool, Sean yelled through his tears, "I hate you! I hate you! I hate you!" The image was of some professional athlete, but my friend wasn't concerned about him. All Sean cared about was the fact that the work of art was meaningful to his dad. What was the cause of his wrath? A few days earlier, Sean's father had announced—at the dinner table—that he was leaving the family for another woman. With that, his dad was gone. A few months later, my friend saw his father driving in a new convertible with the woman, and his wounds only deepened.

Sean and I played basketball every night, and we would talk about how things were going. He wanted more than anything to live a normal life, but his inescapable feelings of bitterness and abandonment were apparent. His younger sister descended into drugs and began sleeping with an older guy, while his mother struggled emotionally. The entire household suffered together through the chaos as they tried to come to grips with the reality that they would have to go on without a father.

It's one thing to lose your dad through an untimely death, such as when a child loses a father who fights in a war to defend his country. The loss is felt, but the memory of the noble dad continues to sustain the child. In time, he or she will experience an acceptance of his absence. However, the fact that Sean's dad *chose* to leave his family left Sean with countless stinging questions: *How long was he lying to us? Why didn't he love us enough to be faithful to mom? How could he create a family only to abandon it?* Even the good memories of his father became a source of further suffering.

The Problem of "Fatherlessness"

Sean's story is not an isolated case. Civilization today—perhaps more than ever—struggles with a crisis of "fatherlessness" in a number of ways. Some men fear the responsibilities of being a dad, so they sterilize themselves or their acts of intercourse. Many of the same men abandon their children after conception occurs. Still others consider children to be an unwanted financial drain, so they urge their pregnant girlfriends to have abortions. They enjoy the act of creating life but don't care to love the life they create. Even if the child survives this gauntlet of threats from a culture of death, only about sixty-five percent of children born out of wedlock live with their biological fathers.[27] Among those, many report that their relationships with their fathers are not close.

It has often been said that many young men bear in their hearts a "father wound." This means that their dads never sufficiently developed and affirmed their manhood. As a result, they constantly feel an urge to prove their manliness to others, while feeling inadequate and hollow inside. As one expert on the subject said, "Until a man knows he's a man, he will be trying to prove that he is one."[28]

One way that some men seek to prove their masculinity is through the sexual conquest of women. However, when the concept of manhood is twisted, fatherhood itself becomes inverted. The aspect of your masculinity that should give life to others ends up destroying them. For example:

- Sexually active girls are more than three times as likely to be depressed as girls who are abstinent.[29] Even if a girl experiments with sex once, research shows an increased risk of depression.[30]

- The rate of suicide attempts for sexually active girls (aged twelve to sixteen) is six times higher than the rate for those girls who have never been sexually active.[31]

I asked one young man who had been sexually active with a number of women if the girls in his past were better off after they had known him. His response? "Yeah, I guess they really got messed up." We men know in our hearts when we have failed to image the love of God to women. Instead of giving life to them, we take it away. We may not intend to do this, and the girl may even initiate the sexual activity. But sometimes a man needs to care for a woman who does not know how to care for herself.

If God chose to reveal himself as "Father," you can be certain that the devil will use every weapon in his arsenal to tarnish the earthly image of fatherhood. Our job is to reverse this cultural plague and restore God's likeness on earth.

The Redemption of Fatherhood

In the Old Testament, a day is promised where the hearts of the fathers would be turned to their children and the hearts of children to their fathers (see Malachi 4:6). Such a promise may strike a nerve for many young men who lack good relationships with their dads. Every young man's situation is unique, but every young man is capable of building a better relationship with his father. Even if his father is no longer living, the son can pray for his father's soul. If the father has abandoned the family, the child can choose to pray and forgive. If the father is living at home but is emotionally distant or verbally abusive, the son can pray, forgive, and attempt to conquer the hardness of his heart with love.

If it doesn't seem that your father's heart is turning toward you, perhaps the promise of God should begin with you. Perhaps your dad desires a deeper relationship with you but assumes you do not feel the same. If you hope to become a father one day, you surely hope to have a close relationship with your children. How will you do this? You will choose to spend time with them and will learn to say the words, "I love you," "I forgive you," and "I'm sorry." Unless a man learns how to do this, he will be incapable of forming an intimate relationship with a child or even with his wife.

Thankfully, you do not need to wait until you are married to practice these skills. The Church calls the family the "school of love" because everything you need to learn about how to love can be learned within your family. After all, if you can love your family members, you are capable of loving anyone on the planet.

> Because you are a son of God, it is your mission to be an image of the Father on earth.

Besides building better relationships within your family, deepen your relationship with the heavenly Father. It has often been said that where your relationship with your dad ends is where your relationship with God begins. In other words, if your father abandoned you, seems detached from you, or demands perfection from you, consider how your attitude toward him mirrors your concept of God. Thankfully, many young men are blessed with exceptional fathers. For them, it is easy to understand a God who is always present, faithful, loving, and strong.

However, if you have not been blessed with such a dad, do not allow this to tarnish your concept of the heavenly Father, who never abandons you and who accepts you as you are. You do not have to earn his love. In the words of St. John Paul II, "We are not the sum of our weaknesses and failures; we are the sum of the Father's love for us and our real capacity to become the image of his Son."[32]

Because you are a son of God, it is your mission to be an image of the Father on earth. By doing so—and by living according to God's plan for you that has been stamped into your own body—you will bring life to the world.

THE MISSION OF THE MAN

If God were to look you in the eyes and ask you, "Who will you be for others?", what would be your response? Your answer to that question will determine the measure of your masculinity.

Ask yourself:

- Do my thoughts, words, and actions toward women speak the truth about who they are? Do I use my God-given strength to serve others, or do I live for myself?

- Do I initiate love with sincerity, or do I initiate relationships based on lust?

- Do I fear the idea of fatherhood, or am I grateful for the gift?

Should you ever lose sight of how to love properly, imagine Jesus hanging upon the Cross and saying to you, "This is how I got my bride to heaven. How else do you think you will get yours there?" The Cross reminds us that sacrifice is the essence of authentic love. Christopher West observes that if newlywed couples looked at the liturgical setting of their weddings, "they would observe that they are pledging themselves *unto death* underneath the corpus of a crucified Bridegroom and right in front of an altar of sacrifice."[33] The same can be said of a seminarian during the rite of his ordination. He is professing with his body that he is laying down his life for his bride, the Church. Whether you are a priest or a husband, having the strength to sacrifice must permeate your vocation.

Although marriage or the priesthood may seem far away, the way you live today will form the person you will become a decade from now. For example, being faithful to a girlfriend now prepares you for the fidelity that will be required of you within your vocation. Likewise, enjoying some years of single life will help you discover, in the words of Blessed Pier Giorgio Frassati, that "one of the most beautiful forms of affection is friendship." If you learn now to use your strength to cherish women and protect life, you will grow in your ability to do what is best for others. If you possess a persevering and committed desire to do what is best for your beloved, you will be well-equipped for the demands of any vocation.

By understanding the design of our bodies and the desires we experience as men, we can understand how God is calling us to live. And by living according to his plan for us, we not only receive the freedom and joy he wishes to offer us, we offer the world a glimpse of God himself. God initiates love and life. He protects, serves, and sacrifices as a manifestation of his strength. He became a living sacrifice and relied upon love as the source of his courage. Not only has he given us the blueprint of manhood, but he has also given us every grace to live in his image and likeness.

The challenges offered in this book are not easy, but as St. John Paul II assures us, "Love supported by prayer is revealed as stronger than death."[34] Through an interior life united with God in prayer, every man is not only capable of following the commandments but is able to become a great saint. Do not be afraid of what this will cost you. Rather, find encouragement in the words of John Paul II, who said, "Every man who seeks the kingdom of God finds himself."[35]

PRAYERS

Jesus, your word says that the eyes of God are ten thousand times brighter than the sun and observe every step a man takes. You know all things, even my most secret thoughts. All too often, I have believed false notions of strength and manhood. My words, thoughts, and actions often show my jaded ideas and selfish motives. Since nothing is hidden from you, I ask you to burn away within me all that is contrary to you. When the beauty of women allures me, help me to recognize my call to love them. When I lose sight of love, call me back to the Cross. Help me to be the kind of man that your daughters deserve. Make my heart generous, noble, and pure. Amen.

St. Joseph, the Church honors you as the Guardian of Virgins. When a man misuses his sexuality, he becomes the opposite: a threat to virgins. You who lived each day by the side of Jesus and Mary, help me to love them as you did, and walk with them through all of my trials. Pray for me now, as you stand now before the throne of God the Father, and guide me to become nothing less than the man he wishes me to become. Amen.

NOTES

1. John Paul II, *Man and Woman He Created Them: A Theology of the Body (TOB)*, translation, introduction and index by Michael Waldstein (Boston: Pauline, 2006), 43:7.
2. TOB 108:5.
3. TOB 13:1.
4. TOB 100:6
5. Christopher West, *Heaven's Song* (West Chester, PA: Ascension, 2008), 49.
6. TOB 109:4.
7. TOB 115:2.
8. TOB 48:1.
9. *Deus Caritas Est* 3.
10. *Deus Caritas Est* 4.
11. West, 86.
12. John Paul II, *Crossing the Threshold of Hope* (New York: Knopf, 1994), 123.
13. West, 45.
14. David Walsh, *Why Do They Act That Way?* (New York: Free Press, 2004), 62.
15. Louann Brizendine, *The Female Brain* (New York: Morgan Road, 2006), 5.
16. TOB 114:4.
17. TOB 13:1; 110:2.
18. St. Josemaria Escriva, *The Way* (New York: Scepter, 2001), 40.
19. Karol Wojtyla, *The Way to Christ* (San Francisco: Harper, 1982), 51.
20. John Paul II, *Crossing the Threshold of Hope*, 124.
21. John and Stasi Eldredge, *Captivating* (Nashville: Thomas Nelson, 2005), 36-37.
22. Bruce Marshall, *The World, the Flesh, and Father Smith* (Boston: Houghton Mifflin, 1945), 108.

23 Wojtyla, 55-56.

24 Wojtyla, 55-56.

25 TOB 21:6.

26 *Gaudium et Spes* 50.

27 US Census Bureau, *Living Arrangements of Children: 2004* (February 2008).

28 John Eldredge, *Wild at Heart* (Nashville: Thomas Nelson, 2001), 62.

29 Robert E. Rector, et al., "Sexually Active Teenagers are More Likely to be Depressed and to Attempt Suicide," The Heritage Foundation (June 3, 2003).

30 Hallfors, et al., "Adolescent Depression and Suicide Risk: Association with Sex and Drug Behavior," *American Journal of Preventive Medicine* 27:3 (October 2004): 224-231; Martha W. Waller, et al., "Gender Differences in Associations Between Depressive Symptoms and Patterns of Substance Use and Risky Sexual Behavior among a Nationally Representative Sample of U.S. Adolescents," *Archives of Women's Mental Health* 9:3 (May 2006): 139-150.

31 D. P. Orr, M. Beiter, G. Ingersoll, "Premature Sexual Activity as an Indicator of Psychological Risk," *Pediatrics* 87 (February 1991): 141-147.

32 John Paul II, Homily, 17th World Youth Day, Toronto (July 28, 2002).

33 West, 145.

34 TOB, general audience of June 27, 1984, paragraph 2, p. 597.

35 Wojtyla, 58.

RESOURCES

Books

   Forged by Jason Evert

   Pure Manhood by Jason Evert

   The Dating Blueprint by Jason Evert

   If You Really Loved Me by Jason Evert

   Male, Female, Other? by Jason Evert

   Pure Faith by Jason Evert

   Pure Love by Jason Evert

   Saint John Paul the Great by Jason Evert

   Theology of the Body in One Hour by Jason Evert

Websites

   chastity.com

ABOUT THE AUTHOR

Jason Evert earned a master's degree in theology and undergraduate degrees in counseling and theology, with a minor in philosophy, at Franciscan University of Steubenville. He is the author of more than fifteen books, including *How to Find Your Soulmate Without Losing Your Soul, The Dating Blueprint,* and *Saint John Paul the Great.* He has spoken on six continents to more than two million teens in high schools and colleges internationally, challenging young people to embrace the virtue of chastity. He runs the website Chastity.com and is the founder of Chastity Project, which is an international alliance of young people who promote chastity in more than forty countries.